handcrafted

TECHNIQUES AND DESIGNS FOR
CUSTOM JEWELRY COMPONENTS

wire findings

denise peck
jane dickerson

INTERWEAVE.
interweave.com

Editor
Anne Merrow

Technical Editor
Bonnie Brooks

Art Director
Liz Quan

Cover + Interior Design
Lee Calderon

Beauty Photography
Joe Coca

Step Photography
Jim Lawson

Photostylist
Ann Sabin Swanson

Production
Katherine Jackson

Interweave Press LLC
201 East Fourth Street
Loveland, CO 80537-5655 USA
Interweave.com

Printed in China by Asia Pacific Offset Ltd.

Library of Congress Cataloging-in-Publication Data

Dickerson, Jane.
  Handcrafted wire findings : techniques and designs for custom
jewelry components / Jane Dickerson, Denise Peck.
      p. cm.
  Includes bibliographical references and index.
  ISBN 978-1-59668-283-2 (pbk.)
  ISBN 978-1-59668-496-6 (eBook)
  1. Wire jewelry. I. Peck, Denise. II. Interweave Press. III. Title.
TT212.D536 2010
739.27--dc22
                           2010032463

10 9 8 7 6 5 4 3 2 1

contents

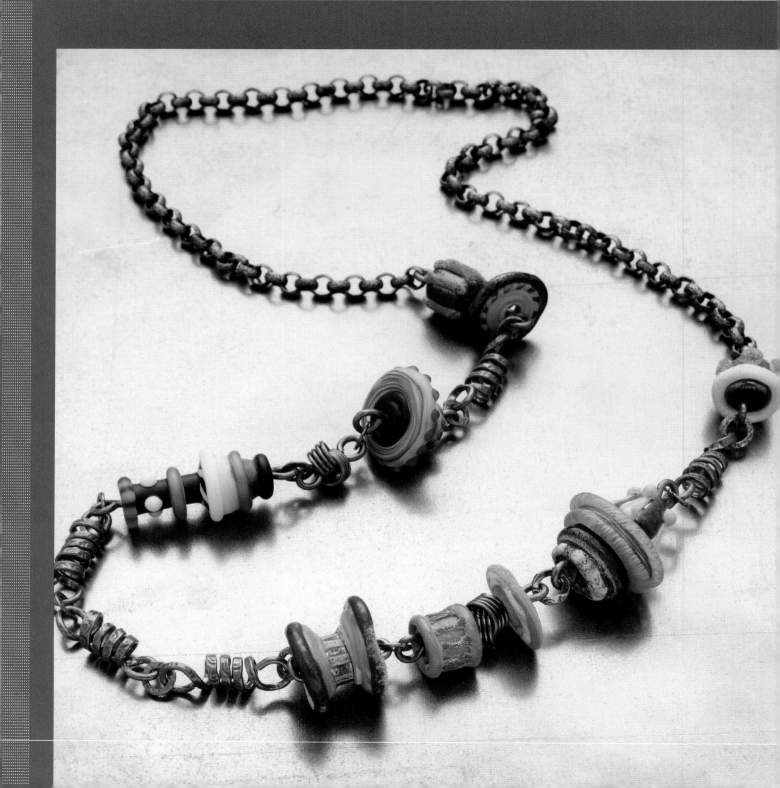

introduction

Findings are the elements that connect, attach, close, or join jewelry pieces together. The most common ones are clasps and ear wires, but the term also includes head pins, charms, links, bead caps, jump rings, bails, and more. A jewelry maker simply can't live without them.

When you find yourself at the end of creating a piece of jewelry and it's time to pick the clasp, the choice can make or break a design. There are so many times when this simple decision is underestimated, but it couldn't be more important. Sometimes a simple S-hook clasp works better than an ornate one, so the investment doesn't need to be expensive. But taking the time to pick the right finding is well worth it.

Many of us have relied on commercially produced findings that are available everywhere you turn. But well-designed handcrafted findings can become your signature as a designer, complementing and enhancing a piece and stylishly finishing it off. A fabulous finding can transform jewelry and become the focal point of the design.

When selecting a finding, you'll find three basic types: functional, decorative, and hybrid. Functional jewelry findings serve a mechanical purpose such as attaching.

Because these components are mechanical, their appearance is less critical, and they're fairly straightforward. They include pin backs, crimps, earring clips and posts, and screw backs.

Decorative jewelry findings are often handmade and are intended to add beauty to the piece. These include charms, pendants, and decorative bails.

Hybrid jewelry findings blend both function and design: bead caps, chain, textured and decorative rings and connectors, coiled links, and beautiful clasps. These components serve a mechanical function as well as contribute to the overall design of the piece.

In this book, we will show you how to make a beautiful collection of handmade decorative and hybrid findings. They are fun to make and most of them only take a few minutes. It is such an advantage for jewelry makers to know how to complete a piece with their own components. Not only is it cost effective, but it also adds one-of-a-kind appeal to your beautifully crafted jewelry. It means you'll never be caught without that last little thing you need to complete your masterpiece!

wire basics

One of the best things about working with wire is that it's such a forgiving medium. If you make a mistake, you can often restraighten the wire and begin again.

Wire comes in a large variety of metals, shapes, and sizes. The size or diameter of the wire is known as the gauge. In the United States, the standard is Brown & Sharpe, also known as American Wire Gauge (AWG). The diameter of wire in inches or millimeters is translated into a numeral from 0 to 34; the higher the number, the thinner the wire. The projects in this book use 10- to 24-gauge round wire.

Wire also comes in a variety of shapes, including round, half-round, twisted, and square. Round is most commonly used and easily available. Half-round wire has a flat side and is commonly used for ring shanks. Square wire has four flat sides, and twisted wire is formed by twisting two round wires together.

Additionally, wire is offered in three hardnesses: dead soft, half hard, and full hard. Dead-soft wire is best if you'll be manipulating it a lot because wire work-hardens as you work with it. Work-hardening stiffens the wire and makes it harder to bend. Eventually it can become so brittle that it can break with additional manipulation. If you are weaving, coiling, or spiraling, you should work with dead-soft wire, because it's much easier on the hands. If you're making ear wires or not planning on working the wire too much, start with half-hard wire, which is already

Photo of different wires—silver, copper, twisted, different gauges.

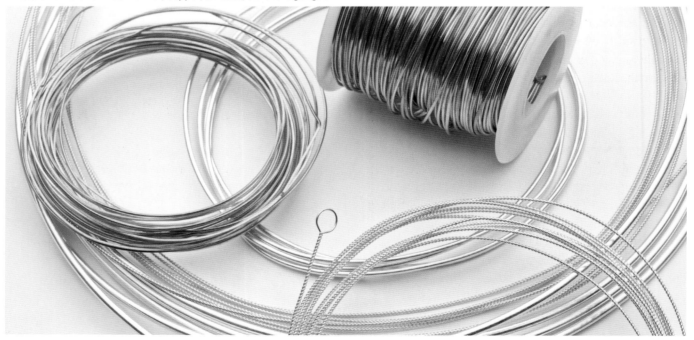

stiffer than dead soft. There are no projects in this book that call for full-hard wire.

You can make findings out of both base-metal and precious-metal wire. The most common base-metal wire used is copper, though aluminum, nickel silver, brass, and bronze are also available. Copper, brass, and colored craft wire are available in hardware and craft stores. All of them can produce finished pieces every bit as beautiful as sterling silver and gold.

Sterling silver, fine silver, and gold wire are precious metals. Sterling silver is 92.5 percent silver mixed with 7.5 percent copper. It is available in several hardnesses and, because of the copper, it tarnishes. Fine silver is 99.9 percent pure silver and is only available in dead soft. Two advantages of fine silver are that it is very malleable and doesn't tarnish. However, because it is so soft, it needs to be work-hardened by hammering or tumbling in steel shot to retain its shape. Fine silver melts at 1,761°F (961°C) and is ideal for fusing or balling up the ends of the wire. Gold wire is expensive, and the cost is often prohibitive, so a common alternative is gold-filled wire, which is a base-metal wire covered with an outer layer of gold. Gold-filled wire is preferable to gold-plated wire because gold plating scratches and wears off easily.

When the directions refer to "working from the spool," it means from a piece of wire one foot or longer (if the length is not specified in the materials list or instructions). You may only need a few inches, and working from the spool instead of cutting a separate length to start each piece eliminates waste and is much more cost-effective.

gauge	round	half-round	square
2g	⬤	◖	◼
3g	⬤	◖	◼
4g	⬤	◖	◼
6g	⬤	◖	◼
7g	●	◖	◼
8g	●	◖	◼
9g	●	◖	◼
10g	●	◖	◼
11g	●	◖	◼
12g	●	◖	◼
13g	●	◖	◼
14g	●	◖	◼
16g	●	◖	◼
18g	•	–	▪
19g	•	–	▪
20g	•	–	▪
21g	•	–	▪
22g	•	–	▪
24g	•	–	▪
26g	·	–	·

tools

Many of the designs in this book require only a few simple tools: a set of pliers, wire cutters, a ring mandrel, and stepped forming pliers (often called wrap-and-tap pliers). As you become more adept at jewelry making, you may want to expand your toolbox to include some of the tools below. In particular, you'll find many of the projects in this book use a micro torch. Tool prices reflect the quality of the tools you're buying and range from very inexpensive to very expensive.

general

General tools range from basic necessities such as flush cutters to mandrels for forming and gauges for measuring.

WIRE GAUGE

The size or diameter of the wire is known as the gauge. Gauge also refers to the tool used to measure wire. Known as the Brown & Sharpe wire gauge, this tool looks a bit like a flat, round gear. It measures the diameter of your wire and is an essential tool for wire jewelry making. A pocket gauge can also be helpful.

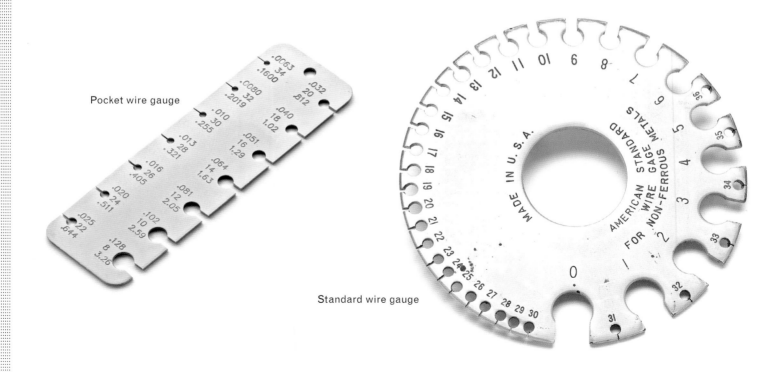

Pocket wire gauge

Standard wire gauge

FLUSH CUTTERS

These are also called side cutters because the cut is made to the side. They have pointed, angled jaws that allow very close cuts in tight places. One side of the jaws is almost flat, the other is concave. Always hold the flat side of the cutters against your work and the concave side against the waste. The flat side creates a nice flush end on your work. Flush cutters are sold with a maximum gauge-cutting capacity; be sure to use cutters that can accommodate the wire you're using.

MANDRELS

A mandrel is a spindle, rod, or bar around which you can bend metal or wire. Mandrels come in a variety of shapes and sizes. Some are made specifically for bracelets, rings, and making bezels. Almost anything can be used as a mandrel to shape wire, including wooden dowels, ballpoint pens, and other pieces of wire. A Sharpie is the perfect shape for making French ear wires.

Mandrels

Pen and Sharpie

Flush cutters

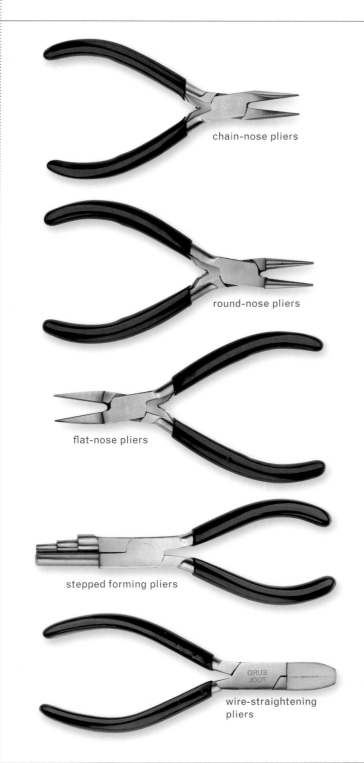

chain-nose pliers

round-nose pliers

flat-nose pliers

stepped forming pliers

wire-straightening
pliers

pliers

There are many varieties of pliers on the market. A good set of pliers will be the best investment you can make. These basics are all you need to make the projects in this book.

CHAIN-NOSE PLIERS
The workhorse of wire tools, chain-nose pliers are like needle-nose pliers, but without teeth that can mar your wire. They are used for grasping wire, opening and closing jump rings, and making sharp angled bends. It's a good idea to have at least two pairs in your workshop.

ROUND-NOSE PLIERS
Another wireworker's necessity, round-nose pliers have pointed, graduated round jaws. They are used for making jump rings, simple loops, and curved bends in wire.

FLAT-NOSE PLIERS
Flat-nose pliers have broad, flat jaws and are good for making sharp bends in wire, grasping spirals, and holding components.

STEPPED FORMING PLIERS
Forming pliers come in different sizes and shapes. Stepped forming pliers have one chain-nose, concave jaw and one jaw of various-sized round barrels. They're perfect for wrapping loops of consistent size. They may also be called wrap-and-tap pliers.

WIRE-STRAIGHTENING PLIERS
These are also called nylon-jaw pliers because the jaws are made of hard nylon. Pulling wire through the clamped jaws will straighten any bends or kinks. They can also be used to hold, bend, or shape wire without marring the metal. Keep in mind that every time you pull wire through

straightening pliers, you're work-hardening it more, making it more brittle and harder to manipulate.

hammering tools

These are used to flatten wire, add texture, and work-harden. Supplemental tools such as an awl, used with a hammer, can pierce holes in wire.

RAWHIDE MALLET
A hammer made of rawhide, this can be used on metal and wire without marring it. It's good for tapping wire into place or for hardening wire.

BALL-PEEN HAMMER
Another staple in the studio, this hammer has one round domed head and one round flat head. The domed head is used for making little dents for texture, while the flat head is used for flattening wire.

AWL
This common household tool comes in handy in a wire studio. A very sharp pointed tool, an awl often has a wooden or acrylic ball for a handle. Use it with a hammer to punch holes in flattened wire.

STEEL BENCH BLOCK
A bench block provides a small and portable hard surface on which to hammer wire. It's made of polished steel and is usually only ¾" (1.9 cm) thick and a few inches square. Use a bench block with a ball-peen hammer for flattening or texturing wire.

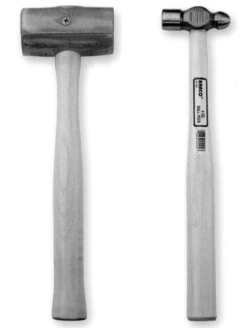

Rawhide mallet   Ball-peen hammer

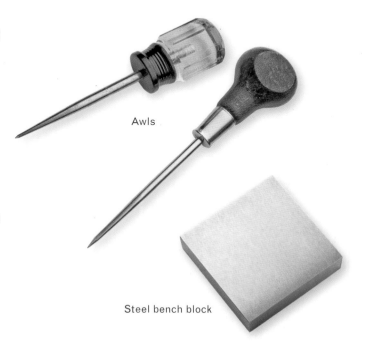

Awls

Steel bench block

fusing and flameworking tools

Introducing fire to your jewelry making might seem scary at first, but it adds decorative and functional touches to your findings that can't be beat.

BLAZER MICRO TORCH
A handheld butane torch has a fine-point adjustable flame that reaches a temperature up to 2,500°F (1,371°C). There are a couple of key features to look for; a flame adjuster and a sturdy base that allows hands-free use are key. Torches with all-metal nozzles tend to be better because extended use can melt any plastic parts near the flame. Some models come with a safety switch, which you might consider, especially if you have children in the house. To protect your eyes, wear flame safety goggles. Most micro torches have a burn time of about 30 minutes on one tank of fuel. Fuel for the torch costs about $4 a can. It's recommended that you buy butane fuel that is triple refined and sold with the torch or at jewelry-supply stores. Lighter fuel may clog the torch and result in an uneven flame.

Tip: Refueling the torch before each use ensures that you will have the hottest flame.

SOLDERING BLOCK & SOLDERITE PAD
A soldering block, charcoal block, or Solderite pad provides a flame-resistant surface for use with a torch. It will protect your work surface from burning. The charcoal block reflects heat back onto the piece for faster fusing and soldering.

QUENCHING BOWL
Any bowl filled with cold water can be used to quickly reduce the heat of an item that has been fused.

FUSING PLIERS
These are everyday needle-nose pliers with a heat-resistant handle. They are not used for jewelry making but for holding wire in the flame when fusing and to dip items in the quenching bowl.

Fusing pliers

Micro torch

Soldering block and Solderite pad

Quenching bowl

finishing tools

These are used to smooth sharp wire ends, alter the wire color, and buff your findings to the perfect shine.

LIVER OF SULFUR
Liver of sulfur is a chemical traditionally used to darken silver wire. It comes in a liquid or solid chunk form and is used for oxidizing, or antiquing, wire. When a small amount is mixed with hot water, it will turn a piece of wire dipped in it from blue to gray to black. Very fine steel wool can be used to finish oxidized silver.

CUP BUR
A cup bur is a tiny cup-shaped file. When you twirl the end of an ear wire inside the cup bur, it smooths and files away all the sharp edges. (It may also be called a wire smoother.)

POLISHING CLOTH
Jewelry polishing cloths are infused with a polishing compound and can be used for cleaning wire, eliminating tarnish, and hardening wire—pulling wire through the cloth repeatedly will stiffen, or work-harden, it. Pro-Polish pads are one of the most popular brands.

NEEDLE FILES
Needle files are made for smoothing sharp ends of metal and wire. They're small and fine and come in different shapes for different purposes. A flat needle file is often all you need for smoothing wire ends.

ROTARY TUMBLER
Often associated with rock tumbling, this same electrical piece of equipment can be used to polish wire and metal jewelry. The barrel must be filled with a tumbling medium such as stainless steel shot (available from jeweler's suppliers) and water. The tumbling action against the shot polishes the metal or wire to a high shine. The tumbling action also helps work-harden, or stiffen, the wire.

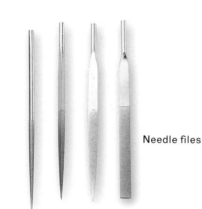

Needle files

Liver of sulfur

Polishing cloth

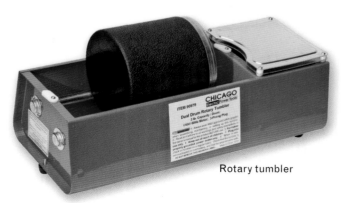

Rotary tumbler

techniques

There are several basic techniques required to make wire jewelry. Over and above those, it's basically just tweaking a bit. If you can learn to make a nice round loop with your round-nose pliers, you're halfway there! Polishing and oxidizing can add a finishing touch.

The secret to fine wire jewelry is neatness. Ends should be neat and smooth or tucked out of sight.

basics

USING A WIRE GAUGE

Brown & Sharpe or AWG (American Wire Gauge) is the standard in the United States for measuring the diameter of wire. When you use a wire gauge, use the small slots around the edge of the gauge, not the round holes at the ends of the slots. Place the wire edge into a slot *(fig. 1)*. If there's wiggle room, place it into the next smaller slot. When you reach a slot that it will not fit into, then the number at the end of the next larger slot is the gauge of your wire.

Fig. 1

FLUSH CUTTING

Flush cutters have two sides: a flat side and a concave side. When you cut wire, you want the end that remains on your working piece to be flat, or flush. To do this, make sure the flat side of the cutters is facing your working piece when you snip.

STRAIGHTENING WIRE

Pulling a piece of wire through nylon-jaw pliers will straighten any bends in the wire. Grasp one end of the wire tightly in the nylon jaws and pull with your other hand *(fig. 1)*. It may take two or three pulls through the pliers to straighten the wire completely. Be aware that the manipulation of wire in any pliers, including nylon-jaw pliers, will start the process of work-hardening the wire, which will eventually make it stiffer and harder to work with.

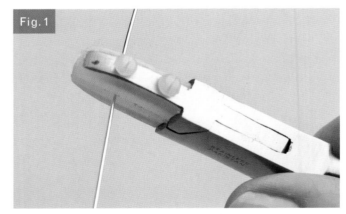

Fig. 1

HAMMERING

Always grasp the hammer firmly near the end of the handle. Do not "choke up" on the handle as you might a baseball bat. This ensures you're using the weight of the head optimally and also keeps your hand from absorbing the shock of the impact.

torch techniques

USING A MICRO TORCH

Micro torches, which are widely available online and in hardware stores, all tend to burn at around the same temperature, 2,500°F (1,371°C) *(fig. 1)*. This temperature is hot enough for fusing fine silver wire as well as a lot of soldering tasks. When you're using a micro torch, it's important to keep the torch filled in order to get the highest heat from it. If it starts to take noticeably longer to heat and melt the metal or solder, refill the torch. The melting point for copper, fine silver, and sterling silver are well below the maximum temperature, making this the perfect tool for fusing and soldering. Always follow the manufacturer's instructions for safety when using a torch.

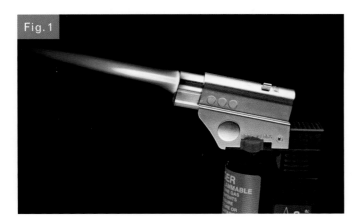

Fig. 1

QUENCHING

Whenever you are using a torch to heat or fuse metal, dip it in a quenching bowl before touching it *(fig. 1)*. Even if a piece is not glowing, a quick dip in a bowl of water will ensure that you're not burned.

Fig. 1

BALLING

Using fusing pliers or tweezers, hold one end of a piece of copper, sterling, or fine silver wire perpendicular in the blue, hottest portion of the flame on the butane torch *(fig. 1)*. When the wire balls up to the size you desire, remove it from the flame and quench it in a bowl of cool water. Copper and sterling will require that you remove the oxidation caused by the flame with a little steel wool *(fig. 2)*.

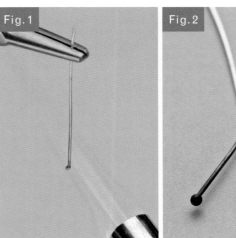

Fig. 1

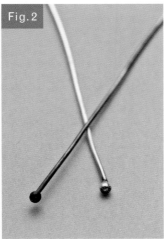

Fig. 2

FUSING

The fusing projects in this book use fine silver, which can be joined without solder or flux. The most fundamental rule of fusing is that you must heat the entire piece, not just the join where the two metal ends meet *(fig. 1)*. Focusing on the join alone results in just burning away the metal there. Instead, slowly and methodically rotate the torch around the entire piece until it's all very hot, then focus on the join to fuse the fine silver. Then immediately pull the flame away *(fig. 2)*.

To join separate pieces of fine silver, it may be necessary to hold them together while the torch is applied. Flux (which is used with solder to fuse metal alloys) or even ordinary household honey can be used to hold pieces in place for fusing. Use a toothpick to apply a small amount of honey or flux to the surface of one piece *(fig. 3)*, then place the second piece where you'd like it to be attached permanently. Heat the entire piece, then focus the flame on the pieces to be joined. The flame will cause the honey or flux to burn away, leaving the pieces fused together *(fig. 4)*.

Fig. 1

Fig. 3

Fig. 2

Fig. 4

ANNEALING

Annealing means heating wire or metal to a temperature where it becomes soft and malleable. When you work with any metal for a time, it will eventually become stiffer and harder to bend. That's called work-hardening. You can restore that malleability with a torch. Run the flame back and forth several times along the length of wire you want to soften. (Wire is so thin that it doesn't need to glow in order to become annealed.) Use pliers to transfer it to a bowl of cold water to quench it before touching it.

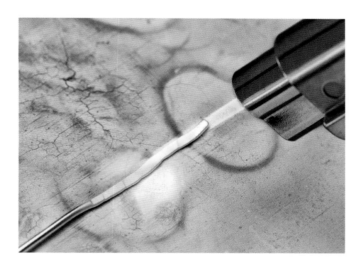

coils and spirals

Coils and spirals are great decorative additions. String a coil of wire onto a straight wire for an extra bit of detail on a project. Spirals can be added to head pins, ear wires, dangles, and more.

COILING

Coils can be made on any round mandrel, including another piece of wire. Hold one end of the wire tightly against the mandrel with your thumb and coil the length up the mandrel. Be sure to wrap snugly and keep the coils right next to one another *(fig. 1)*. Flush cut both ends *(fig. 2)*.

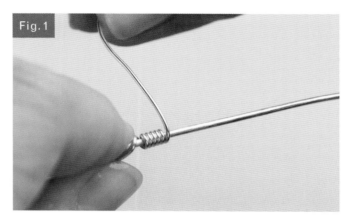

Fig. 1

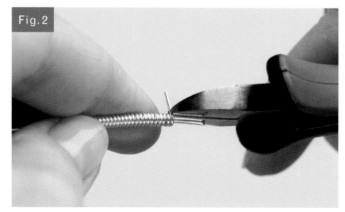

Fig. 2

SPIRALING

Make a very small loop with round-nose pliers *(fig. 1)*. Grasp the loop in flat-nose pliers and use the thumb of your other hand to push the wire around the loop *(fig. 2)*. Continue to move the spiral around in the jaws of the flat-nose pliers to enable you to enlarge the coil *(fig. 3)*.

Fig. 1

Fig. 2

Fig. 3

jump rings

Jump rings are used to connect components or as design elements.

MAKING JUMP RINGS

Coil wire snugly around a mandrel *(fig. 1)*. Each single coil will make one jump ring. Remove the mandrel. Use flush cutters to cut through all the rings at the same spot along the length of the coil, snipping one or two at a time *(fig. 2)*. They will fall away and each ring will be slightly open *(fig. 3)*. Note that one side of the ring will be flush cut and the other side will have a beveled edge. Flush cut the beveled side so the ring will close properly. The jump rings you make will have the inner diameter (ID) of the mandrel you used to make them.

Fig. 1

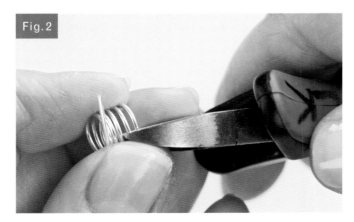

Fig. 2

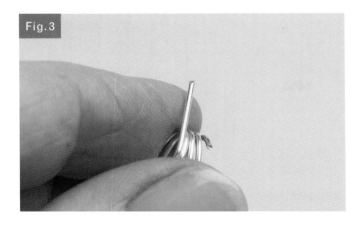

Fig. 3

Tip: When purchasing jump rings, note that some vendors sell them by inner diameter measurements and some vendors sell them by outer diameter measurements. The difference is minuscule and only essential if you're working on a complex chain mail design.

OPENING AND CLOSING JUMP RINGS

Always use two chain- or bent-nose pliers to open and close jump rings. Grasp the ring on each side of the opening with pliers *(fig. 1)*. Gently push one side away from you while pulling the other side toward you, so the ring opens from side to side *(fig. 2)*. To close, reverse the directions of your hands.

Fig. 1

Fig. 2

head pins

You can make head pins with almost any kind of wire in almost any gauge. The most important aspects are that they are the right diameter to go through the beads you've chosen and that they're long enough for the bead or stack of beads you want to string. Keep in mind that you must have ¾" (2 cm) to 1½" (3.8 cm) beyond the beads to make a loop with the wire. You can make a slew of head pins ahead of time, in varying lengths and gauges, and you can also make them as you need them. The four versions here include a balled end, a pinched end, a flattened end, and a spiraled end.

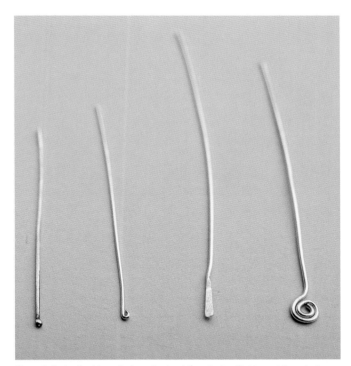

From left, balled head pin, pinched head pin, flattened head pin, spiraled head pin

BALLED HEAD PIN

Make a small loop on the end of 1"–3" (2.5–7.5 cm) of wire. Hold the nonlooped wire end with the fusing pliers and place the looped end into the micro torch flame. When the wire balls up to the size you desire, remove it from the flame and quench it in a bowl of cool water.

PINCHED HEAD PIN

This is the quickest and easiest head pin to make. Using any wire, bend one end up 1/16" (1.5 mm) and pinch it snugly against the length of the wire.

FLATTENED HEAD PIN

Using any wire, hold one end of the wire against your steel bench block and hammer 1/8" (3 mm) flat with a ball-peen hammer.

SPIRALED HEAD PIN

Using any wire, make a tiny loop at the end of the wire with the smallest end of round-nose pliers *(fig. 1)*. With chain- or flat-nose pliers, hold the loop you just made flat in the jaws and use the thumb of your other hand to push the long wire around the loop to form a spiral *(fig. 2)*. When the spiral is the size you want, use your chain- or flat-nose pliers to bend the remaining wire out from the spiral at a 90° angle.

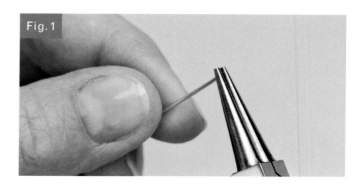

Fig. 1

Fig. 2

ear wires

Making ear wires is one of the simplest techniques with the greatest benefits. First, it saves you from having to buy them—and they can be costly. Second, it allows you to personalize your earrings right down to the ear wires, in whatever design you want. Every head pin you just learned to make can be made into a custom ear wire!

BASIC EAR WIRES

Make a small loop on the end of 1½" (3.8 cm) of wire *(fig. 1)*. Hold the loop against a Sharpie marker and bend the wire over the marker away from the loop *(fig. 2)*. Use round-nose pliers to make a small bend outward at the end of the wire *(fig. 3)*. Use a cup bur or file to smooth the end of the wire.

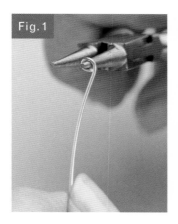

Fig. 1

Fig. 2

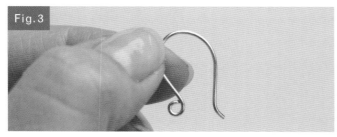

Fig. 3

FLATTENED EAR WIRES

Hammer flat the tip of 1¾" (4.5 cm) of wire *(fig.1)*. Use round-nose pliers to bend up the flattened tip *(fig. 2)*. Hold the loop against a Sharpie marker and bend the wire over the marker away from the loop *(fig. 3)*. Use round-nose pliers to make a small bend outward at the end of the wire. Use a cup bur or file to smooth the end of the wire.

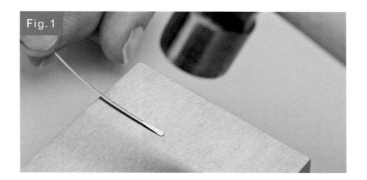

Fig. 1

Fig. 2

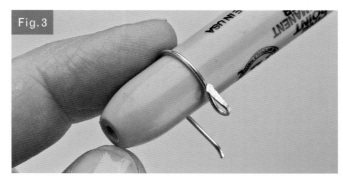

Fig. 3

BALLED EAR WIRES

Ball up the end of 1¾" (4.5 cm) of sterling, copper, or fine silver wire as with balled head pin and quench in water to cool. Use round-nose pliers to make a small loop at the balled end *(fig. 1)*. Hold the loop against a Sharpie marker and bend the wire over the marker away from the loop *(fig. 2)*. Use round-nose pliers to make a small bend outward at the end of the wire. Use a cup bur or file to smooth the end of the wire.

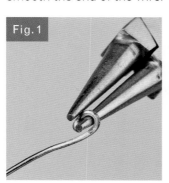

Fig. 1

Fig. 2

SPIRALED EAR WIRES

Create a spiral at the end of 1¾" (4.5 cm) of wire *(fig. 1)*. Hold the spiral flat in your chain-nose pliers and bend the wire perpendicular to the spiral *(fig. 2)*. Hold the spiral against a Sharpie marker and bend the wire over the marker away from the spiral *(fig. 3)*. Pinch the spiral against the finished ear wire. Use round-nose pliers to make a small bend outward at the end of the wire. Use a cup bur or file to smooth the end of the wire *(fig 4)*.

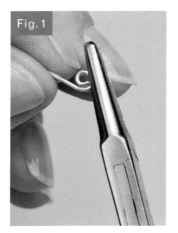
Fig. 1

Fig. 2

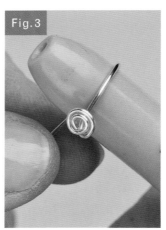
Fig. 3

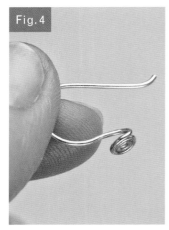
Fig. 4

loops

Loops are secure connections between elements.

SIMPLE LOOP

Grasp the end of the wire in round-nose pliers so you can just see the tip of the wire *(fig. 1)*. Rotate the pliers fully until you've made a complete loop *(fig. 2)*. Remove the pliers. Reinsert the tip of the pliers to grasp the wire directly across from the opening of the loop. Make a sharp 45° bend across from the opening *(fig. 3)*, centering the loop over the length of the wire like a lollipop *(fig. 4)*.

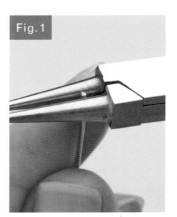
Fig. 1

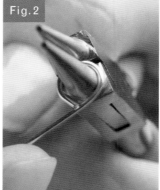
Fig. 2

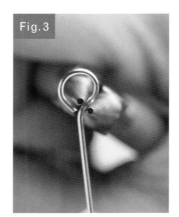
Fig. 3

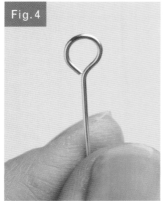
Fig. 4

WRAPPED LOOP

Grasp the wire about 2" (5 cm) from the end with chain-nose pliers. Use your fingers to bend the wire flat against the pliers to 90° *(fig. 1)*. Use round-nose pliers to grasp the wire right at the bend you just made, holding the pliers perpendicular to the tabletop. Pull the wire up and over the top of the round-nose pliers *(fig. 2)*. Pull the pliers out and put the lower jaw back into the loop you just made *(fig. 3)*. Continue pulling the wire around the bottom jaw of the pliers into a full round loop *(fig. 4)*. With your fingers or chain-nose pliers, wrap the wire around the neck of the lower wire two or three times *(figs. 5–6)*.

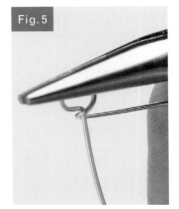

Fig. 5

Fig. 6

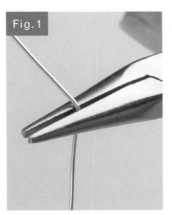

Fig. 1

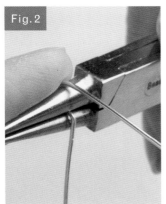

Fig. 2

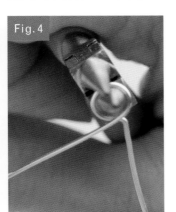

Fig. 3

Fig. 4

BRIOLETTE LOOP

For top-drilled stones, insert a wire through the hole and bend up both sides so that they cross over the top of the stone *(fig. 1)*. (You will only need a short length on one side.) Make a bend in each of the wires so they point straight up off the top of the stone. Use flush cutters to

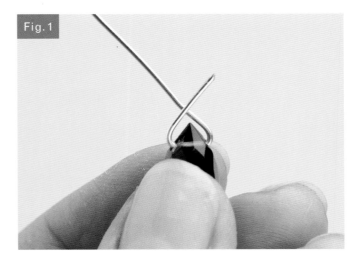

Fig. 1

trim the short wire so that it's no longer than ⅛" (3 mm) *(fig. 2)*. Pinch the two wires together with chain-nose pliers and bend the longer wire over the top of the shorter wire to 90° *(fig. 3)*. Make a wrapped loop by switching to round-nose pliers and pulling the long wire up and over the round jaw *(figs. 4–5)*. Wrap the neck of the two wires together two or three times to secure *(figs. 6–7)*.

piercing and oxidizing

Piercing and oxidizing are fun ways to add additional detail to your earring designs. Small pierced holes turn a piece of wire into a link, a dangle, and more. Oxidizing adds color and dimension to wire.

PIERCING
If wire has been flattened, you can pierce it with an awl to make a hole for connecting other elements, such as ear wires. It's best to work on a scrap piece of wood. Take a sharp awl and position it where you want the hole. Push firmly to make an impression—a starter spot *(fig. 1)*. Then place the point of the awl in the impression and strike the top sharply with a hammer *(fig. 2)*.

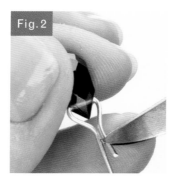
Fig. 2

Fig. 3

Fig. 4

Fig. 5

Fig. 6

Fig. 7

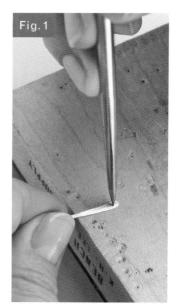
Fig. 1

Fig. 2

OXIDIZING

Liver of sulfur is used to darken, or patina, wire. Dissolve a small lump of liver of sulfur in very hot water. Dip your piece into the solution *(fig. 1)*. Depending on the temperature of the solution and the length of time you leave the piece in it, the wire can turn a variety of colors, including gold, blue, and black *(fig. 2)*. Remove the piece when it reaches the desired color *(fig. 3)*. Dry and polish it lightly to remove some of the patina *(fig. 4)*, but leave the dark color in the recesses of the piece *(fig. 5)*.

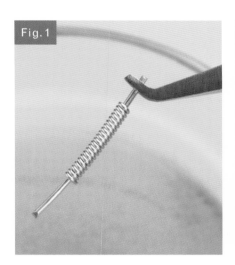

Fig. 1

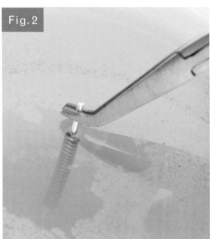

Fig. 2

Fig. 3

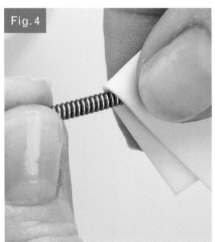

Fig. 4

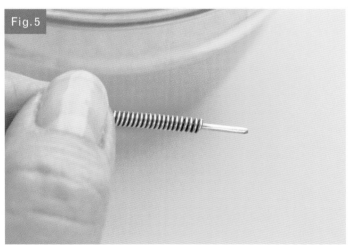

Fig. 5

ear wires

Nothing personalizes your earrings like a handmade pair of ear wires. There's almost nothing simpler, so they're great projects for beginners. You need only a few very basic tools and a few inches of half-hard wire. Remember to smooth the ends of your ear wires for that professional touch.

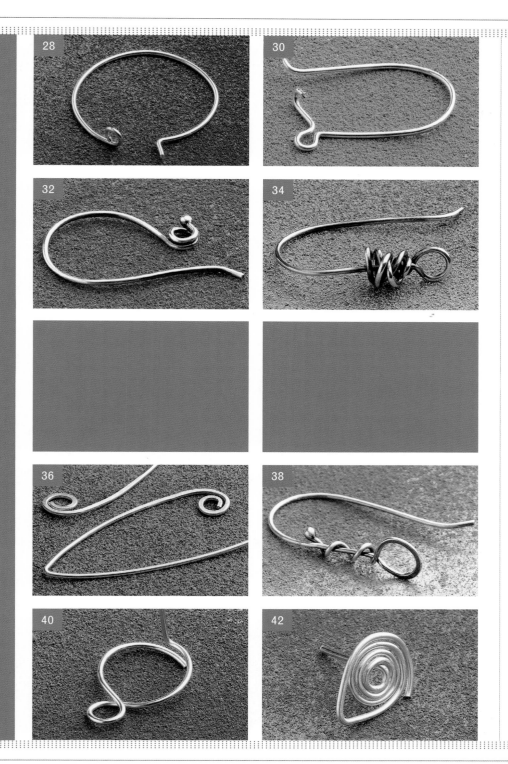

circle loop ear wires

materials + tools

- 7" (18 cm) of 20-gauge sterling silver half-hard wire
- Ruler
- Flush cutters
- Ring mandrel
- Round-nose pliers
- Chain-nose pliers
- File or cup bur
- Polishing cloth or rotary tumbler with mixed stainless steel shot

Finished size: 7/8" (2.2 cm) diameter

1 Cut 3½" (9 cm) of wire and flush cut both ends. Place the middle of the wire against the size 10 mark on the ring mandrel and wrap the ends of the wire in opposite directions to form a circle *(Fig.1)*.

Fig.1

2 Use the tip of the round-nose pliers to make a P-shaped loop on one end of the wire *(Fig. 2)*.

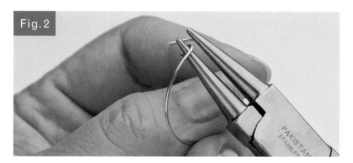
Fig.2

3 Put the ear wire back on the mandrel at size 10. Use chain-nose pliers to bend the other end of the wire opposite the loop up at a 90° angle *(Fig. 3)*.

Fig.3

4 Remove the ear wire from the mandrel and trim the end to ⅛" (3 mm) *(Fig. 4)*. Use the file or cup bur to round and smooth the end of the wire *(Fig. 5)*.

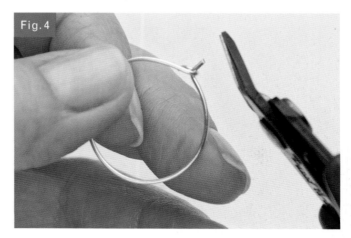
Fig.4

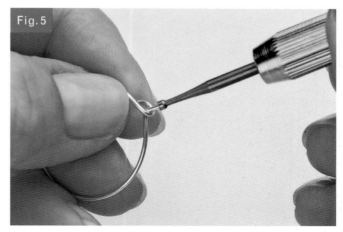
Fig.5

5 Put the ear wire back on the ring mandrel if it needs reshaping.

6 Repeat Steps 1–5 for the other ear wire. Polish for a high shine.

kidney ear wires

materials + tools

- 5½" (14 cm) of 20-gauge sterling silver half-hard wire
- Ruler
- Flush cutters
- Round-nose pliers
- Sharpie marker
- File or cup bur
- Polishing cloth or rotary tumbler with mixed stainless steel shot

Finished size: ⅝" x 1" (1.5 x 2.5 cm)

1 Cut 2¾" (7 cm) of wire and flush cut both ends. Make a 90° bend ¾" (2 cm) from one end of the wire with round-nose pliers *(Fig. 1)*.

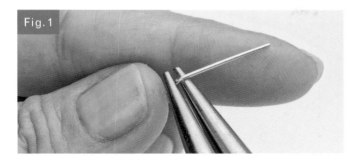
Fig. 1

2 With the tip of the round-nose pliers, grasp the short side of the wire right next to the bend. Bend the short end of the wire over the tip of the pliers until it touches the long wire *(Fig. 2)*.

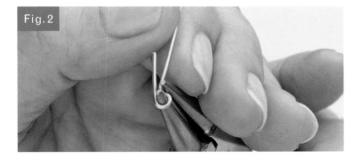
Fig. 2

3 Insert the round-nose pliers into the loop and bend the short wire back to a 90° angle *(Fig. 3)*. Using the tip of the round-nose pliers, grasp the end of the short wire and bend it back on itself to form a small hook *(Fig. 4)*.

Fig. 3

Fig. 4

4 Place the Sharpie at the middle of the long wire and bend the wire over the marker to form a hook *(Fig. 5)*. Use round-nose pliers to bend the end of the wire up slightly *(Fig. 6)*. Use the file or cup bur to round and smooth the end of the wire.

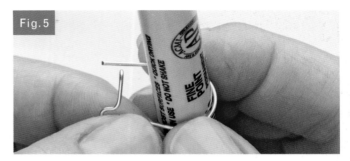
Fig. 5

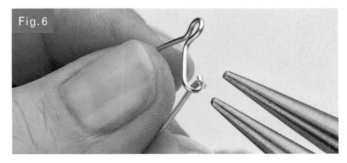
Fig. 6

5 Repeat Steps 1–4 for the other ear wire. Polish for a high shine.

double-loop french ear wires

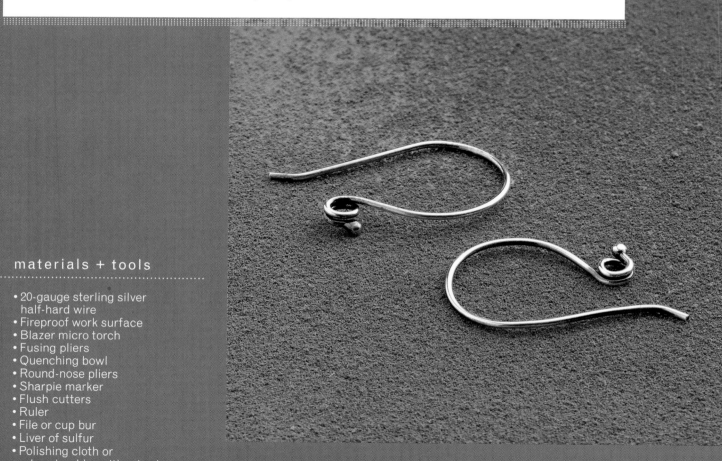

materials + tools

- 20-gauge sterling silver half-hard wire
- Fireproof work surface
- Blazer micro torch
- Fusing pliers
- Quenching bowl
- Round-nose pliers
- Sharpie marker
- Flush cutters
- Ruler
- File or cup bur
- Liver of sulfur
- Polishing cloth or rotary tumbler with mixed stainless steel shot

Finished size: ½" x1" (1.4 x 2.5 cm)

1 On a fireproof work surface, light the torch. Working from the spool, use fusing pliers to hold the end of the wire in the flame until a ball forms *(Fig. 1)*. Turn off the torch. Dip the wire in the quenching bowl to cool, then dry.

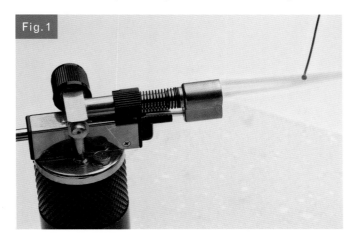
Fig. 1

2 Grasp the wire just beneath the ball with the tip of the round-nose pliers. Wrap the wire around the jaw twice, making a double loop *(Fig. 2)*. Bend the wire over the Sharpie to make a hook *(Fig. 3)*.

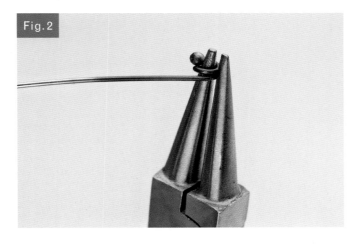
Fig. 2

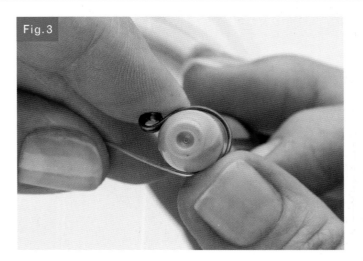
Fig. 3

3 Cut the wire off the spool to the desired length. Use round-nose pliers to bend the end of the wire up slightly *(Fig. 4)*. Use the file or cup bur to round and smooth the end of the wire. Oxidize with liver of sulfur if desired.

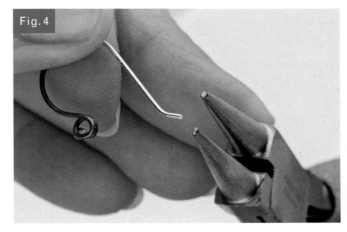
Fig. 4

4 Repeat Steps 1–3 for the other ear wire. Polish for a high shine.

tumbleweed french ear wires

materials + tools

- 20-gauge sterling silver dead-soft wire
- Flush cutters
- Chain-nose pliers
- Ruler
- Sharpie marker
- Round-nose pliers
- File or cup bur
- Liver of sulfur
- Rotary tumbler with mixed stainless steel shot

Finished size: ½" x 1" (1.3 x 2.5 cm)

1 Working from the spool, flush cut the end of the wire, then use chain-nose pliers to make a 90° bend 3½" (9 cm) from the end of the wire *(Fig. 1)*.

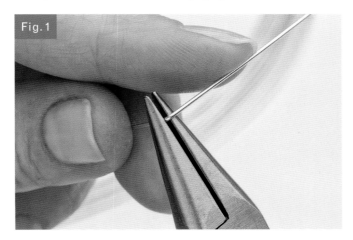

2 Create a wrapped loop and continue wrapping to use up all of the short wire *(Fig. 2)*. Use chain-nose pliers to tuck in the end of the wire.

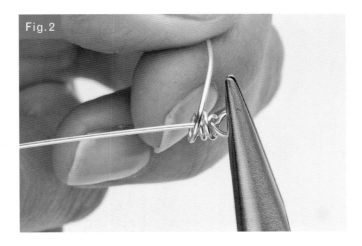

3 Bend the wire over the Sharpie to form a hook *(Fig. 3)*. Cut to length. Use round-nose pliers to bend the end of the hook up slightly *(Fig. 4)*. Use the file or cup bur to round and smooth the end of the wire.

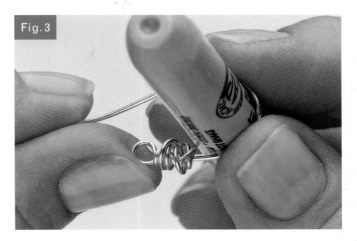

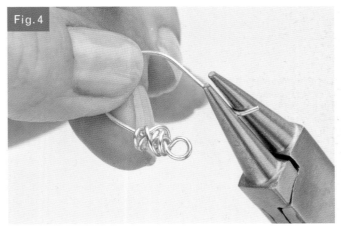

4 Repeat Steps 1–3 for the other earring. Oxidize with liver of sulfur, then tumble to polish and work-harden.

fiddlehead ear wires

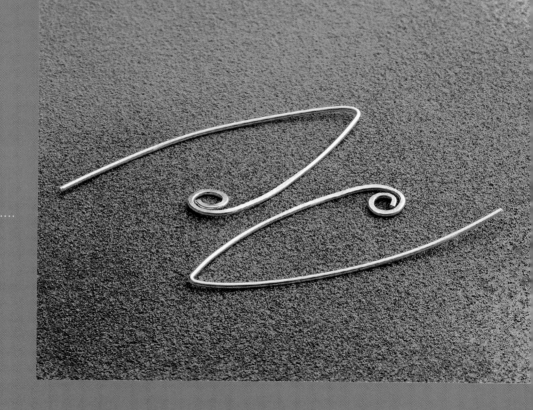

materials + tools

- 20-gauge sterling silver half-hard wire
- Flush cutters
- Round-nose pliers
- Ruler
- Chain-nose pliers
- File or cup bur
- Ball-peen hammer
- Steel bench block
- Polishing cloth or rotary tumbler with mixed stainless steel shot

Finished size: ⅔" x 1⅔" (1.7 x 4.3 cm)

1 Working from the spool, flush cut the end of the wire. Use the tip of the round-nose pliers to make a small loop *(Fig. 1)*; spiral around a second time *(Fig. 2)*.

2 Measure 1¼" (3.2 cm) from the spiral and make a hairpin turn with chain-nose pliers *(Fig. 3)*. Cut the wire off the spool 1¾" (4.5 cm) from the bend.

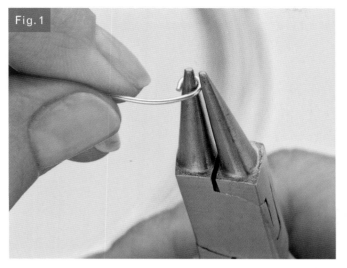

Fig. 1

Fig. 2

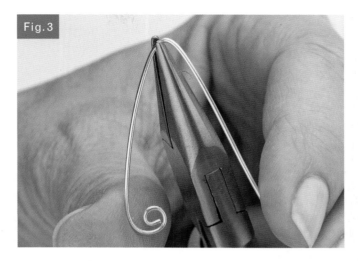

Fig. 3

3 Use a file or cup bur to round and smooth the end of the ear wire.

4 Use the hammer and bench block to flatten the spiral and ½" (1.3 cm) up from the spiral *(Fig. 4)*.

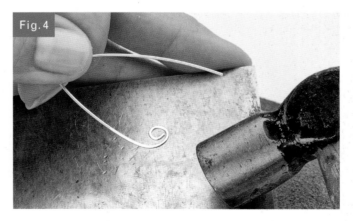

Fig. 4

5 Repeat Steps 1–4 for the other ear wire. Polish for a high shine.

vine ear wires

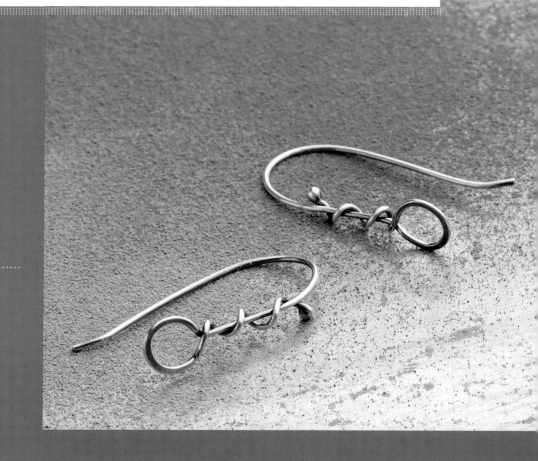

materials + tools

- 20-gauge sterling silver half-hard wire
- Fireproof work surface
- Blazer micro torch
- Fusing pliers
- Quenching bowl
- Ruler
- Round-nose pliers
- Sharpie marker
- Flush cutters
- File or cup bur
- Ball-peen hammer
- Steel bench block
- Liver of sulfur
- Rotary tumbler with mixed stainless steel shot
- 0000 steel wool

Finished size: ½" x 1⅛" (1.3 x 2.8 cm)

1 On a fireproof work surface, light the torch. Working from the spool, use fusing pliers to hold the end of the wire in the flame until a ball forms *(Fig. 1)*. Turn off the torch. Dip the wire in the quenching bowl to cool, then dry. Remove the oxidization caused by the flame with steel wool.

Fig. 1

2 Grasp the wire 1¼" (3.2 cm) from the ball with the back of the round-nose pliers *(Fig. 2)*. Make a complete loop *(Fig. 3)* and twist the short end of the wire up the neck of the spool wire *(Fig. 4)*.

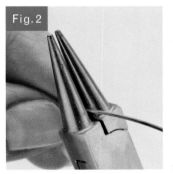

Fig. 2

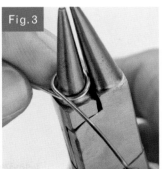

Fig. 3

Fig. 4

3 Place the Sharpie ¾" (2 cm) from the top of the loop and fold the wire over the marker to form a hook *(Fig. 5)*. Cut the wire off the spool just below the loop *(Fig. 6)*. Use round-nose pliers to bend the end of the wire up slightly. Use the file or cup bur to round and smooth the end of the wire.

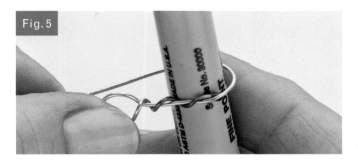

Fig. 5

Fig. 6

4 Use the hammer and bench block to hammer the loop flat *(Fig. 7)*.

Fig. 7

5 Repeat Steps 1–4 for the other ear wire. Oxidize with liver of sulfur, then tumble to polish and work-harden.

circle post ear wires

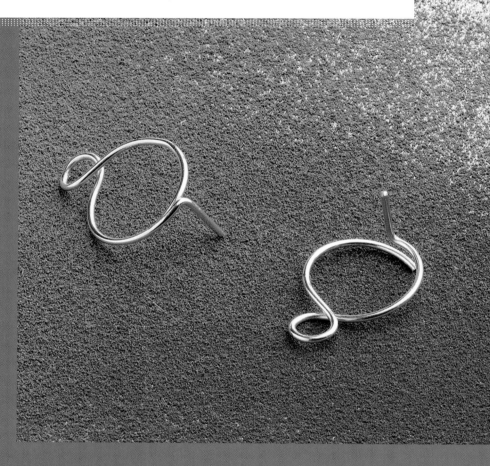

materials + tools
....

- 5½" (14 cm) of sterling silver 20-gauge half-hard wire
- Flush cutters
- Round-nose pliers
- Stepped (5, 7, 10 mm) forming pliers
- Chain-nose pliers
- Ruler
- File or cup bur
- Polishing cloth or rotary tumbler with mixed stainless steel shot

Finished size: ½" x ¾" (1.3 x 2 cm)

1 Cut the wire in half. Place the middle of one piece of wire about one-third of the way down the jaw of the round-nose pliers *(Fig. 1)*. Bend the wire around the jaw of the pliers to make a loop, with the ends forming a straight line *(Fig. 2)*.

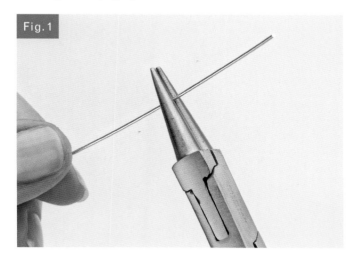

Fig. 1

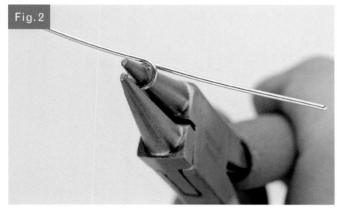

Fig. 2

2 Grasp the wire right next to the loop with the large (10 mm) step on the stepped pliers. The stepped jaw of the pliers should be facing you, and the loop should face away from you, on the left side of the pliers. Push both wires around the jaw of the pliers in opposite directions as far as they will go *(Fig. 3)*.

Fig. 3

3 Grasp the straight wire at the top of the large circle with chain-nose pliers and bend the wire straight back to form the post *(Fig. 4)*. Trim the inner wire 1/8" (3 mm) *(Fig. 5)*. Use the file or cup bur to round and smooth the end of the post.

Fig. 4

Fig. 5

4 Repeat Steps 1–3, except the loop made in Step 2 should be facing away from you on the right side of the pliers to create a mirror image. Polish for a high shine.

spiral post ear wires

materials + tools

- 20-gauge sterling silver
  half-hard wire
- Flush cutters
- Ruler
- Chain-nose pliers
- Round-nose pliers
- Flat-nose pliers
- File or cup bur
- Polishing cloth or
  rotary tumbler with mixed
  stainless steel shot

Finished size: ⅜" x ½" (1 x 1.3 cm)

1 Working from the spool, flush cut the end of the wire, then make a 90° bend with the chain-nose pliers ¾" (2 cm) from the end of the wire *(Fig. 1)*. Using round-nose pliers, begin making a spiral with the wire from the spool *(Fig. 2)*.

Fig. 1

Fig. 2

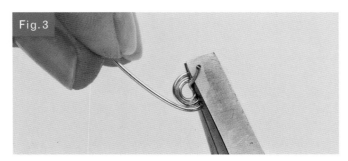

2 After 1½ rotations, hold the spiral flat in the flat-nose pliers and continue for 3 full rotations *(Fig. 3)*. As you come around the bottom of the ear wire on your fourth rotation, hold the point of the chain-nose pliers on the wire and bend it to a 45° angle *(Fig. 4)*.

Fig. 3

Fig. 4

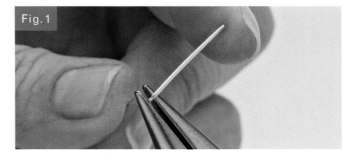

3 Finish the fourth spiral around the top of the ear wire and trim the wire on the side *(Fig. 5)*. Trim the post to ½" (1.3 cm). Use the file or cup bur to round and smooth the end of the ear wire.

Fig. 5

4 Repeat Steps 1–3, spiraling the wire in the opposite direction for the other ear wire. Polish for a high shine.

links & connectors

Links and connectors are a great way to lengthen necklaces and bracelets. Make up a few at a time so you'll always have some on hand when your piece calls for a special design element. Some links are so distinctive, you can use them all by themselves as beautiful earrings—or make them large to create a great focal point for a necklace.

fused oval links

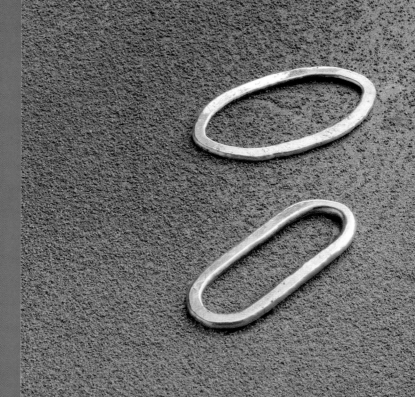

materials + tools

- 14-gauge fine silver dead-soft wire
- Ring mandrel
- Flush cutters
- File
- Fireproof work surface
- Soldering block
- Blazer micro torch
- Fusing pliers
- Quenching bowl
- Rawhide or nylon mallet
- Round-nose pliers
- Ball-peen hammer
- Steel bench block
- Rotary tumbler with mixed stainless steel shot

Finished size: Varies

1 Working from the spool, use the ring mandrel to make a jump ring in size 3 *(Fig. 1)*. Flush cut and file the ends of the wire so they meet with no gap when the ring is closed *(Fig. 2)*.

Fig. 1

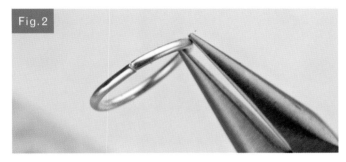
Fig. 2

2 On a fireproof work surface, place the ring on the soldering block and light the torch. Holding the torch about 1½" (3.8 cm) from the ring, rotate the flame around the ring, slowly heating the whole surface. When the ring glows, concentrate the flame on the join until it flows together *(Fig. 3)*. Turn off the torch. Use fusing pliers to dip the ring in the quenching bowl to cool, then dry.

Fig. 3

3 Reshape the ring on the mandrel with a rawhide or nylon mallet *(Fig. 4)*.

Fig. 4

4 Place the ring over the tips of the round-nose pliers and open the pliers to stretch the ring into the desired shape *(Fig. 5)*.

Fig. 5

5 Use the hammer and bench block to flatten the ring *(Fig. 6)*.

Fig. 6

6 Tumble to polish and work-harden.

decorative fused link

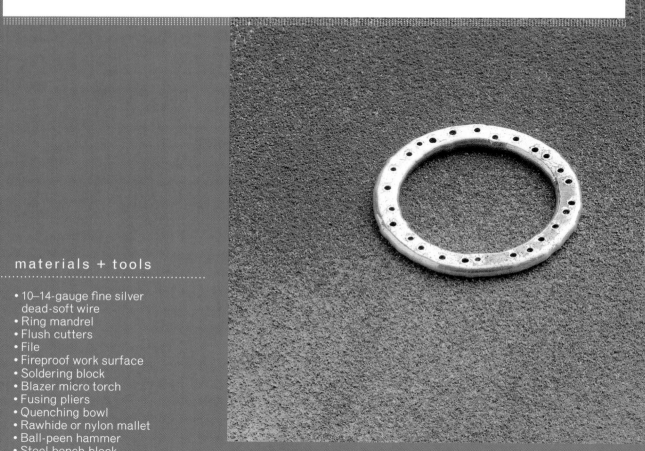

materials + tools

- 10–14-gauge fine silver dead-soft wire
- Ring mandrel
- Flush cutters
- File
- Fireproof work surface
- Soldering block
- Blazer micro torch
- Fusing pliers
- Quenching bowl
- Rawhide or nylon mallet
- Ball-peen hammer
- Steel bench block
- Transparent packing tape
- Metal stamp, texturizing hammer, or awl
- Liver of sulfur
- Rotary tumbler with mixed stainless steel shot
- Optional: Sharpie pen, polishing cloth

Finished size: 1" (2.5 cm)

1 Working from the spool, wrap the wire around the size 5½ mark on the ring mandrel to make a jump ring. Flush cut and file the ends of the wire so they meet with no gap when the ring is closed *(Fig. 1)*.

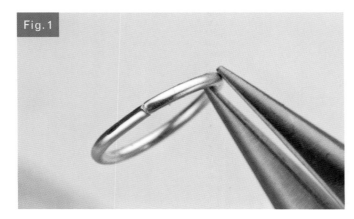
Fig. 1

2 On a fireproof work surface, place the ring on the soldering block and light the torch. Holding the torch about 1½" (3.8 cm) from the ring, rotate the flame around the ring in a circle, slowly heating the whole surface. When the ring glows, concentrate the flame on the join until it flows together *(Fig. 2)*. Turn off the torch. Use fusing pliers to dip the ring in the quenching bowl to cool, then dry.

Fig. 2

3 If necessary, reshape the ring on the mandrel using a rawhide or nylon mallet.

4 Use the hammer and bench block to hammer the ring flat.

5 Tape the ring to the bench block to hold it in place. Texturize the ring through the tape with the ball-peen hammer and texturizing tool (a metal stamp, a texturizing hammer, or an awl) *(Fig. 3)*. Repeat for the other side.

Fig. 3

6 Oxidize with liver of sulfur if desired. Tumble to polish and work-harden. Alternatively, in place of liver of sulfur, cover the piece with black ink from the Sharpie, then polish it off with a polishing cloth, leaving the dark color in the recesses.

hammered ring connector

materials + tools

- 10-gauge fine silver dead-soft wire
- Ring mandrel
- Flush cutters
- File
- Fireproof work surface
- Soldering block
- Blazer micro torch
- Fusing pliers
- Quenching bowl
- Rawhide or nylon mallet
- Ball-peen hammer
- Steel bench block
- Hole punch
- Liver of sulfur
- Rotary tumbler with mixed
  stainless steel shot

Finished size: 1⅛" (2.8 cm)

1 Working from the spool, wrap the wire around the size 5½ (14 cm) mark on the ring mandrel to make a jump ring. Flush cut and file the ends of the wire so they meet with no gap *(Fig. 1)*.

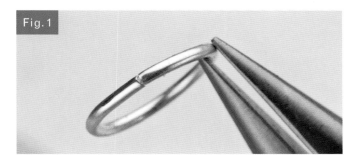
Fig. 1

2 On a fireproof work surface, place the ring on the soldering block and light the torch. Holding the torch about 1½" (3.8 cm) from the ring, rotate the flame around the ring in a circle, slowly heating the whole surface. When the ring glows, concentrate the flame on the join until it flows together *(Fig. 2)*. Turn off the torch. Use fusing pliers to dip the ring in the quenching bowl to cool, then dry.

Fig. 2

3 Place the ring on the mandrel to reshape, using the rawhide or nylon mallet to gently bring it back to round.

4 Use the hammer and bench block to flatten the ring *(Fig. 3)*.

Fig. 3

5 Place the ring on the soldering block and light the torch. Heat the ring to anneal it, or until it glows. This will make the silver softer and more malleable. Use fusing pliers to dip the ring in the quenching bowl to cool, then dry.

6 Using the round head of the ball-peen hammer and the bench block, hammer one side of the ring to create a dimpled texture *(Fig. 4)*.

Fig. 4

7 Punch a hole on opposite sides of the ring with the hole punch *(Fig. 5)*. Oxidize with liver of sulfur if desired. Tumble to polish and work-harden.

Fig. 5

sailor's knot link

materials + tools

- 24-gauge sterling silver twisted wire or 24-gauge copper wire
- Chain-nose pliers
- Ruler
- Round-nose pliers
- Flush cutters
- Liver of sulfur
- Rotary tumbler with mixed stainless steel shot

Finished size: ¼" x ⅝" (6 x 15 mm)

1 Working from the spool, use chain-nose pliers to make a 90° bend 2¾" (7 cm) from the end of the wire *(Fig. 1)*.

Fig. 1

2 Use the middle of the round-nose pliers to create a wrapped loop, wrapping the short wire 4 to 6 times around the neck *(Fig. 2)*. Trim the wire and tuck in the end with chain-nose pliers.

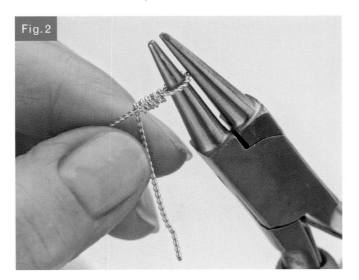

Fig. 2

3 Measure 3½" (9 cm) from the wrap and cut the wire from the spool.

4 Using chain-nose pliers, make a 90° bend on the same plane as the loop, just above the wrap *(Fig. 3)*. Repeat Step 2, wrapping neatly over the first coil *(Fig. 4)*. Trim the wire and tuck in the end.

Fig. 3

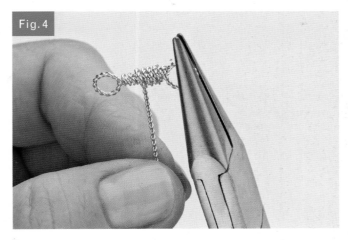

Fig. 4

5 Oxidize with liver of sulfur if desired. Tumble to polish and work-harden.

wired ring link

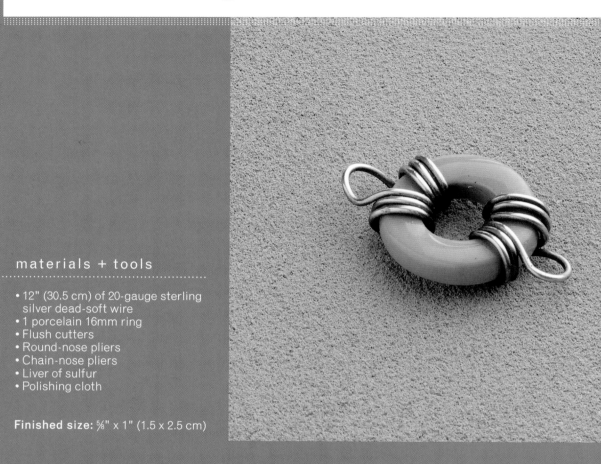

materials + tools

- 12" (30.5 cm) of 20-gauge sterling silver dead-soft wire
- 1 porcelain 16mm ring
- Flush cutters
- Round-nose pliers
- Chain-nose pliers
- Liver of sulfur
- Polishing cloth

Finished size: ⅝" x 1" (1.5 x 2.5 cm)

1 Cut the wire into two 6" (15 cm) lengths. Using round-nose pliers, bend one piece in half and hang the ring on the hairpin bend *(Fig. 1)*.

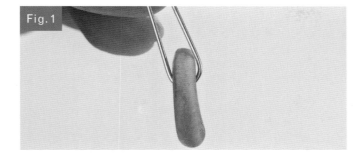

Fig. 1

2 Using your fingers and chain-nose pliers, wrap the back wire twice around the ring from back to front *(Fig. 2)*.

Fig. 2

3 Place the back of the bottom jaw of the round-nose pliers on top of the ring and wrap the front wire over the jaw to form a loop *(Fig. 3)*. Continue wrapping each wire until 3 wraps show on the front on each side *(Fig. 4)*. *Note:* The loop wire counts as one of the wraps.

Fig. 3

Fig. 4

4 Trim the wires on the back of the ring and gently pinch in the ends with chain-nose pliers *(Fig. 5)*. Use round-nose pliers to grasp the loop and twist it to face the front of the ring *(Fig. 6)*.

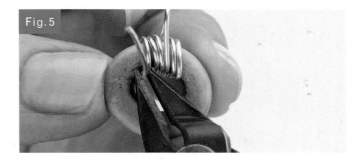

Fig. 5

Fig. 6

5 Repeat Steps 1–4 on the opposite side of the ring.

6 Oxidize with liver of sulfur if desired. Polish with the polishing cloth.

twisted beaded link

materials + tools

- 18–20-gauge sterling silver dead-soft wire
- 24-gauge sterling silver twisted wire
- 3mm decorative bead
- Flush cutters
- Round-nose pliers
- Ruler
- Chain-nose pliers
- Liver of sulfur
- Rotary tumbler with mixed stainless steel shot

Finished size: ¼" x 1" (6 x 25 mm)

1 Working from the spool of 18–20-gauge wire, flush cut the end of the wire, then use round-nose pliers to make a simple loop on the end *(Fig. 1)*.

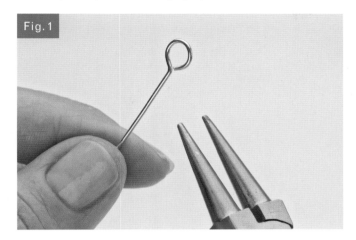

Fig. 1

2 Working from the spool of twisted wire, wrap the twisted wire around the 18–20-gauge wire to make a twisted coil 14 wraps long *(Fig. 2)*. Cut the twisted wire off the coil.

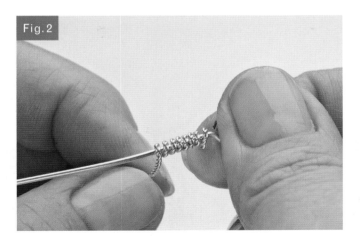

Fig. 2

3 Flush cut the 18–20-gauge wire off the spool 1½" (3.8 cm) from the loop. Remove the coil and cut 2 pieces that are each 5 wraps long *(Fig. 3)*.

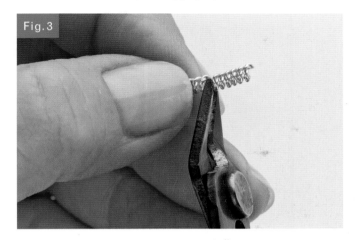

Fig. 3

4 String one coil, the bead, and the second coil onto the piece of 18–20-gauge wire and make a simple loop *(Fig. 4)*. Oxidize with liver of sulfur if desired. Tumble to polish and work-harden.

Fig. 4

textured corkscrew link

materials + tools

- 16-gauge sterling silver
  dead-soft wire
- Ruler
- Sharpie marker
- Flush cutters
- Ball-peen hammer
- Steel bench block
- Fireproof work surface
- Soldering block
- Blazer micro torch
- Fusing pliers
- Quenching bowl
- Transparent packing tape
- Metal stamp
- File
- Stepped (5, 7, 10 mm) forming pliers
- Chain-nose pliers
- 0000 steel wool
- Polishing cloth

Finished size: 5/16" x 1⅛" (8 x 28 mm)

1 Working from the spool, measure ¾" (2 cm) from the end and make a mark *(Fig. 1)*. Measure 3½" (9 cm) from the mark and make a second mark. Measure ¾" (2 cm) from the second mark and cut the wire from the spool. Use the hammer and bench block to flatten between the first and second mark *(Fig. 2)*.

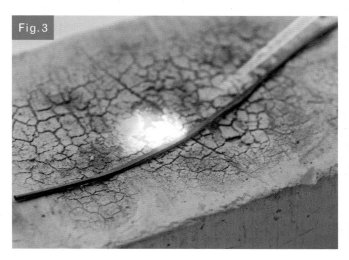
Fig. 3

Fig. 1

3 Tape the wire to the bench block. Use the hammer and metal stamp to texture the flattened section of the wire through the packing tape *(Fig. 4)*. Remove the tape.

Fig. 2

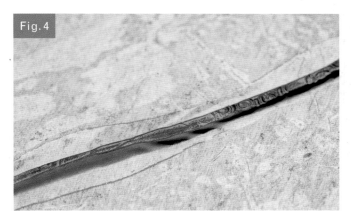
Fig. 4

2 On a fireproof work surface, place the wire on the soldering block and light the torch. Heat the wire in the flame to anneal it, or just until it glows *(Fig. 3)*. Turn off the torch. Use fusing pliers to dip the wire in the quenching bowl to cool, then dry.

4 File each end of the wire. Grasp the end of the wire with the small (5 mm) step of the stepped pliers and make a coil with the entire length of wire *(Fig. 5)*.

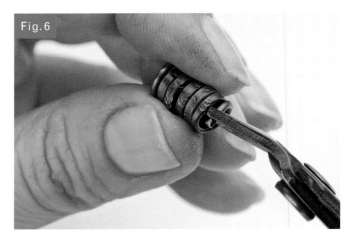

Fig. 6

Fig. 5

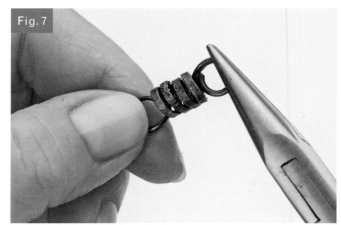

Fig. 7

5 Flush cut each end of the wire directly across from where the texturing starts, leaving one round untextured coil at each end *(Fig. 6)*. Use chain-nose pliers to fold up each round untextured loop so each sits perpendicular to the coil *(Fig. 7)*. Grasp both loops with chain-nose pliers and twist until they are on the same plane *(Fig. 8)*. Hold the coil in your fingers and grasp one loop with chain-nose pliers; pull the core coil apart slightly *(Fig. 9)*. Repeat on the other end of the coil.

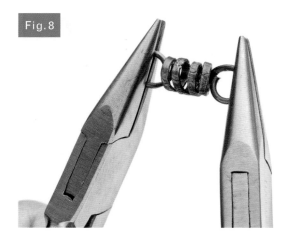

Fig. 8

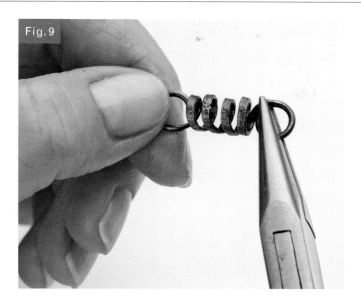

Fig. 9

7 Use the steel wool pad to remove the excess oxidation caused by the torch. Use the polishing cloth to bring out the shine *(Fig. 11)*.

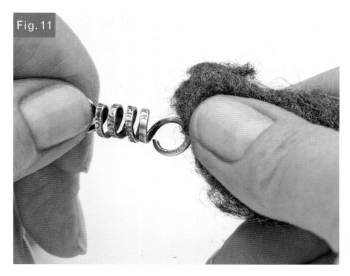

Fig. 11

6 Use the hammer and bench block to flatten the loops on each end of the link *(Fig. 10)*.

Fig. 10

lasso link

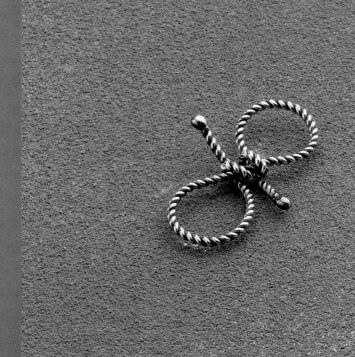

materials + tools

- 22-gauge sterling silver twisted wire
- Ruler
- Stepped (5, 7, 10 mm) forming pliers
- Flush cutters
- Chain-nose pliers
- Fireproof work surface
- Blazer micro torch
- Fusing pliers
- Quenching bowl
- 0000 steel wool
- Rotary tumbler with mixed stainless steel shot

Finished size: ⅜" x 1" (1 x 2.5 cm)

1 Working from the spool, grasp the wire 1½" (3.8 cm) from the end with the second (7 mm) step of the stepped pliers. Cross the wires around the barrel to form a loop *(Fig. 1)*.

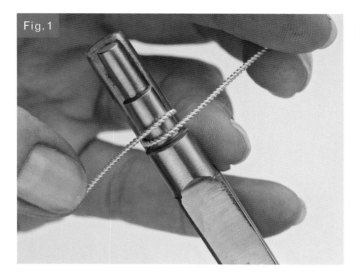
Fig. 1

2 Grasp the spool wire right next to the loop with the same step of the pliers. Make a second loop, forming a figure-eight *(Fig. 2)*. Cut the wire off of the spool, leaving 1" (2.5 cm).

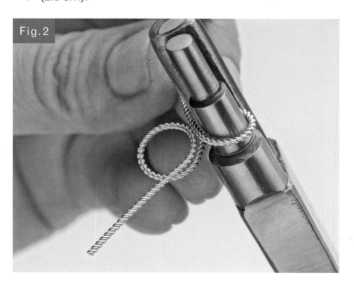
Fig. 2

3 Grasp one loop flat in the jaws of the chain-nose pliers and use your fingers to wrap the end wire of that loop once around the neck *(Fig. 3)*. Repeat with the other wire. Trim the ends of the wire to ⅜" (1 cm).

Fig. 3

4 On a fireproof work surface, light the torch. Use the fusing pliers to hold the link in the flame. Heat the entire piece to blacken it, then concentrate the flame on one end of the wire until it forms a ball *(Fig. 4)*. Use fusing pliers to dip the link in the quenching bowl to cool. Turn the link over and ball the other end of the wire. Quench. Turn off the torch.

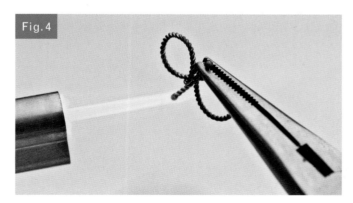
Fig. 4

5 Dry the link, then remove the excess oxidation with steel wool. Tumble to polish and work-harden.

figure-eight link

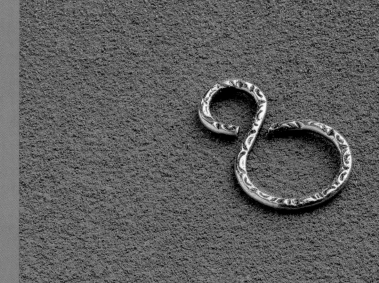

materials + tools

....

- 16-gauge sterling silver
  dead-soft wire
- Flush cutters
- Round-nose pliers
- Ballpoint pen
- Transparent packing tape
- Steel bench block
- Ball-peen hammer
- Metal stamp
- Liver of sulfur
- Rawhide or nylon mallet
- Polishing cloth or rotary tumbler
  with mixed stainless steel shot

Finished size: ½" x ¾" (1.3 x 2 cm)

1 Working from the spool, flush cut the end of the wire, then make a P-shaped loop two-thirds of the way down the round-nose pliers *(Fig. 1)*.

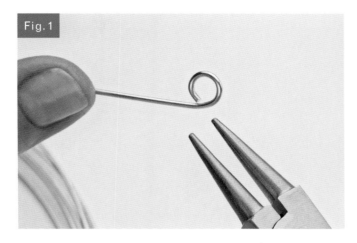

Fig. 1

2 Place the pen above the loop and wrap the wire around the pen until it crosses over at the top of the small loop *(Fig. 2)*. Flush cut the spool wire where the circle is complete *(Fig. 3)*.

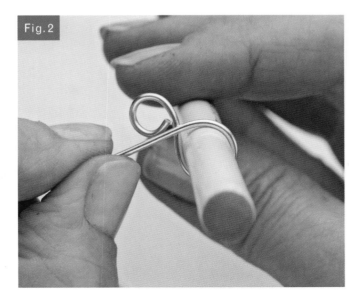

Fig. 2

Fig. 3

3 Tape the link to the bench block. Use the ball-peen hammer, metal stamp, and bench block to add texture to one side of the link *(Fig. 4)*. Remove the tape. Reshape the link with round-nose pliers, if necessary.

Fig. 4

4 Oxidize with liver of sulfur. Use the rawhide or nylon mallet and bench block to hammer the link a few times to work-harden or tumble to polish and work-harden.

yin-yang link

materials + tools

- 18-gauge sterling silver dead-soft wire
- Flush cutters
- Ruler
- Round-nose pliers
- Flat-nose pliers
- Ball-peen hammer
- Steel bench block
- Liver of sulfur
- Rotary tumbler with mixed stainless steel shot

Finished size: 7⁄16" x 1" (1.1 x 2.5 cm)

1 Working from the spool, flush cut the end of the wire, then grasp the wire 4" (10 cm) from the end with the tip of the round-nose pliers. Wrap the two wires in opposite directions around both tips, forming a yin-yang shape *(Fig. 1)*.

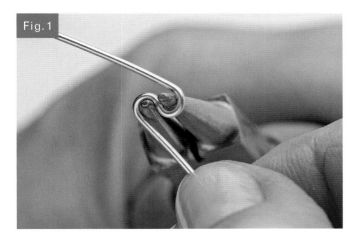

Fig. 1

2 Measure 4" (10 cm) from the yin-yang shape and flush cut the wire from the spool.

3 Hold the yin-yang shape flat with your fingers and alternately spiral the ends around the core until you have 3 full spirals *(Fig. 2)*. Alternatively, use flat-nose pliers if it's easier than holding the wire with your fingers *(Fig. 3)*.

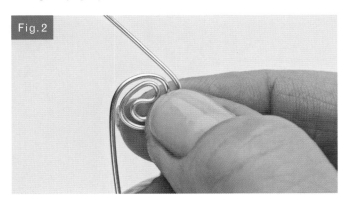

Fig. 2

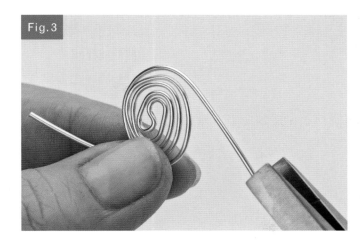

Fig. 3

4 Measuring from the top of the yin-yang spiral, cut the ends to ¾" (2 cm). Use round-nose pliers to make a simple loop on each end *(Fig. 4)*.

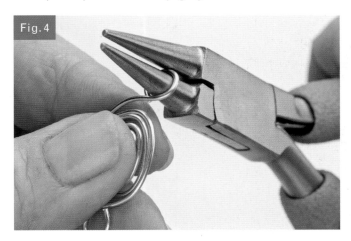

Fig. 4

5 Use the hammer and bench block to flatten the link slightly.

6 Oxidize with liver of sulfur, then tumble to polish and work-harden.

s-hook clasps

This classic design has so many variations and can be dressed up or down depending on your style. Add a beautiful bead to make the clasp the focal point of your design. Simpler ones work well for bracelets, and they always add an artisan's touch. They're deceptively simple to make and the easiest clasp to use.

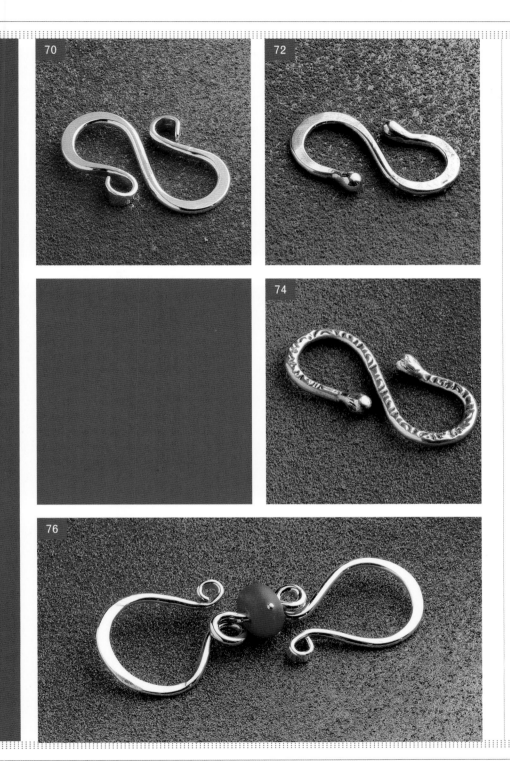

70 Hammered S-Hook Clasp

72 Ball-End Hammered S-Hook Clasp

74 Ball-End Textured S-Hook Clasp

76 S-Hook Clasp with Bead

hammered s-hook clasp

materials + tools

- 2¼" (5.5 cm) of 16-gauge sterling silver dead-soft wire
- Flush cutters
- File or cup bur
- Ball-peen hammer
- Steel bench block
- Round-nose pliers
- Rotary tumbler with mixed stainless steel shot

Finished size: ½" x ⅞" (1.3 x 2.2 cm)

1 Flush cut each end of the wire. Use the file or cup bur to round and smooth the ends.

2 Use the hammer and bench block to flatten ¼" (6 mm) on each end of the wire into a paddle *(Fig. 1)*.

Fig. 1

3 Use the tip of the round-nose pliers to create a small P-shaped loop on the end of each paddle, facing in opposite directions *(Fig. 2)*.

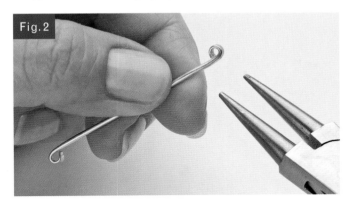

Fig. 2

4 Grasp one end of the wire with the back of the round-nose pliers, just below the loop, with the loop facing you *(Fig 3)*. Rotate the pliers away from you, rolling the wire completely over to form a hook *(Fig. 4)*. Repeat this entire step on the other end of the clasp *(Fig. 5)*.

Fig. 3

Fig. 4

Fig. 5

5 Using the hammer and bench block, flatten the curve of the hook on each side of the clasp *(Fig. 6)*.

Fig. 6

6 Tumble to polish and work-harden.

ball-end hammered s-hook clasp

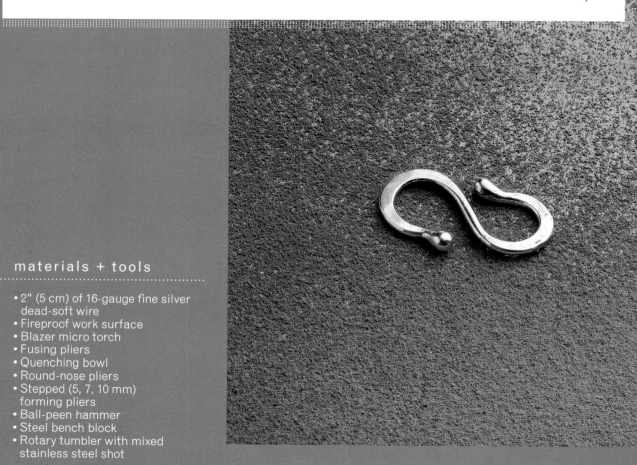

materials + tools

- 2" (5 cm) of 16-gauge fine silver dead-soft wire
- Fireproof work surface
- Blazer micro torch
- Fusing pliers
- Quenching bowl
- Round-nose pliers
- Stepped (5, 7, 10 mm) forming pliers
- Ball-peen hammer
- Steel bench block
- Rotary tumbler with mixed stainless steel shot

Finished size: $\frac{7}{16}$" x $\frac{3}{4}$" (1.1 x 2 cm)

1 On a fireproof work surface, light the torch. Use the fusing pliers to hold one end of the wire in the flame until a ball forms. Dip the wire in the quenching bowl to cool. Repeat this entire step to create a ball on the other end of the wire *(Fig. 1)*. Turn off the torch. Dry the wire.

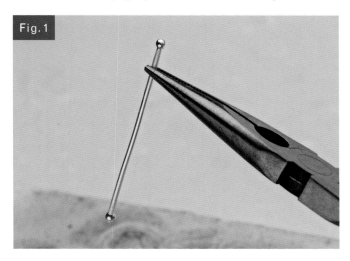

Fig. 1

2 Grasp the wire just beneath the ball with the back of the round-nose pliers *(Fig. 2)*. Rotate the pliers away from you, rolling the wire completely over, forming a hook *(Fig. 3)*. Repeat this step for the other end of the clasp *(Fig. 4)*. Grasp the wire just beneath the ball with the tip of the round-nose pliers and make a slight bend upward; repeat on the other end *(Fig. 5)*.

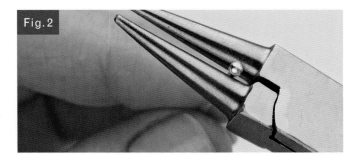

Fig. 2

Fig. 3

Fig. 4

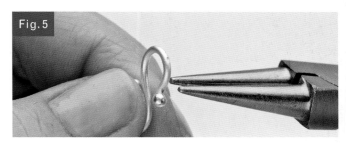

Fig. 5

3 Use the hammer and bench block to flatten the curve of the hook on each side of the clasp *(Fig. 6)*.

Fig. 6

4 Tumble to polish and work-harden.

ball-end textured s-hook clasp

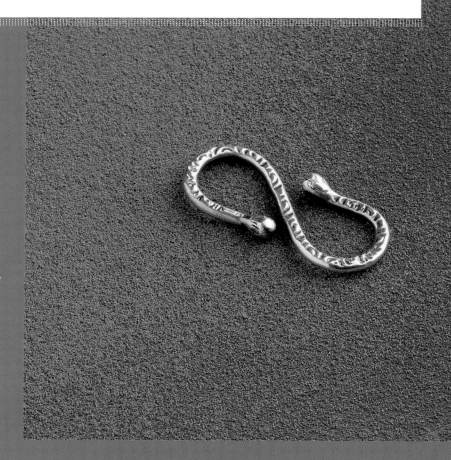

materials + tools

- 2¾" (7 cm) of 14-gauge sterling silver dead-soft wire
- Fireproof work surface
- Blazer micro torch
- Fusing pliers
- Quenching bowl
- Stepped (5, 7, 10 mm) forming pliers
- Transparent packing tape
- Steel bench block
- Ball-peen hammer
- Metal stamp
- Rawhide or plastic mallet
- Liver of sulfur
- Rotary tumbler with mixed stainless steel shot

Finished size: ⁷⁄₁₆" x 1" (1.1 x 2.5 cm)

1 On a fireproof work surface, light the torch. Use the fusing pliers to hold one end of the wire in the flame until a ball forms. Dip the wire in the quenching bowl to cool. Repeat on the other end of the wire *(Fig. 1)*. Quench. Turn off the torch. Dry the wire.

Fig. 1

2 Grasp one end of the wire just below the ball with the second (7 mm) step of the stepped pliers. Rotate the pliers away from you, rolling the wire completely over, forming a hook *(Fig. 2)*. Repeat this entire step on the other end of the clasp *(Fig. 3)*.

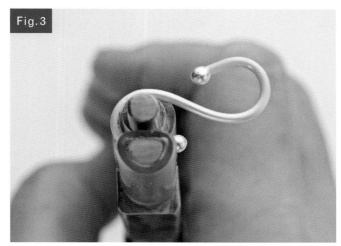

Fig. 2

Fig. 3

3 Tape the clasp to the bench block to keep it in place. Use the ball-peen hammer and metal stamp to make impressions through the tape on one side of the clasp *(Fig. 4)*. Remove the tape. Use the rawhide or nylon mallet to reflatten the clasp if there is any distortion during texturing.

Fig. 4

4 Oxidize with liver of sulfur, then tumble to polish and work-harden.

s-hook clasp with bead

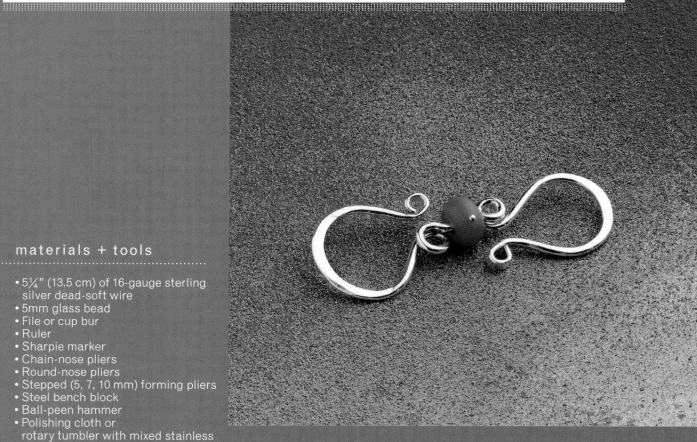

materials + tools

- 5¼" (13.5 cm) of 16-gauge sterling silver dead-soft wire
- 5mm glass bead
- File or cup bur
- Ruler
- Sharpie marker
- Chain-nose pliers
- Round-nose pliers
- Stepped (5, 7, 10 mm) forming pliers
- Steel bench block
- Ball-peen hammer
- Polishing cloth or rotary tumbler with mixed stainless steel shot

Finished size: ½"x 1¾" (1.3 x 4.5 cm)

1 Round and smooth both ends of the wire with the file or cup bur *(Fig. 1)*. Mark the center of the wire at 2⅝" (6.7 cm). String the bead to the center of the mark and mark the wire again on each side of the bead *(Fig. 2)*. Remove the bead.

2 Using chain-nose pliers, make a 90° bend at the top mark *(Fig. 3)*. Use the tip of the round-nose pliers to create a loop that goes 1¼ times around the jaw so that the wire sticks off the loop at a 45° angle *(Fig. 4)*.

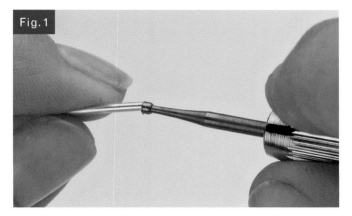

Fig. 1

Fig. 2

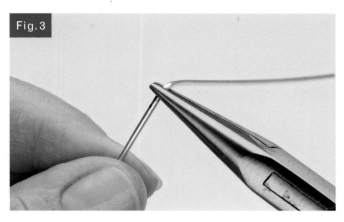

Fig. 3

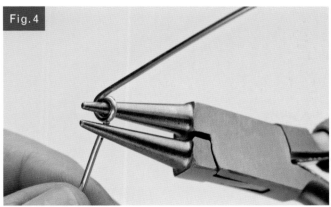

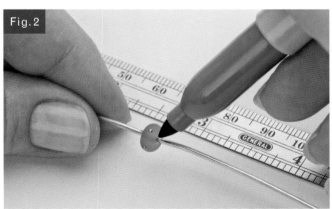

Fig. 4

3 Add the bead and repeat Step 2, but make the 90° bend in the opposite direction for this loop *(Figs. 5–6)*.

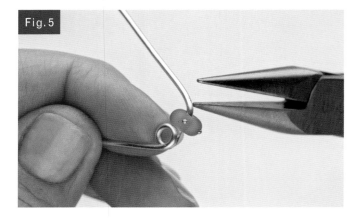

Fig. 5

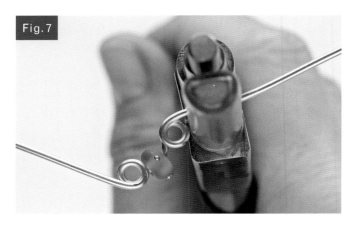

Fig. 7

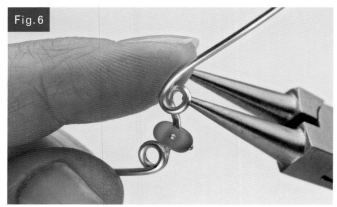

Fig. 6

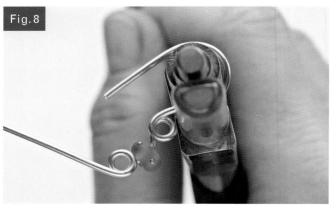

Fig. 8

4 Grasp the wire with the large (10 mm) step of the stepped pliers, holding the bottom (non-step) portion of the pliers next to the loop *(Fig. 7)*. Bend the wire over the jaw of the pliers to form a hook *(Fig. 8)*. Repeat this step on the other end of the wire *(Fig. 9)*.

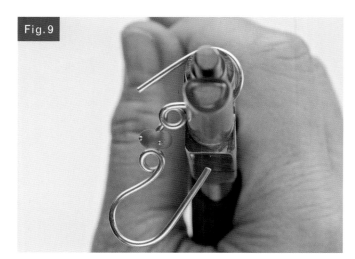

Fig. 9

5 Open one hook slightly and place the wire end against the bench block, holding the loop vertically in your fingers. Use the hammer and bench block to flatten the end of the wire, making a ¼" (6 mm) paddle *(Fig. 10)*. Use the tip of the round-nose pliers to make a loop on the end of the paddle *(Fig. 11)*. Repeat this entire step for the other end of the clasp.

Fig. 10

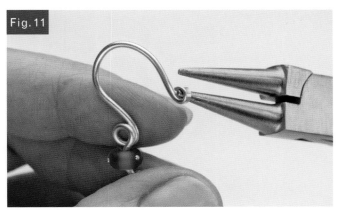

Fig. 11

6 Bend each hook so the loop on the bead and the loop on the hook sit opposite each other *(Fig. 12)*. Use the hammer and bench block to flatten the top of the curve on each side *(Fig. 13)*.

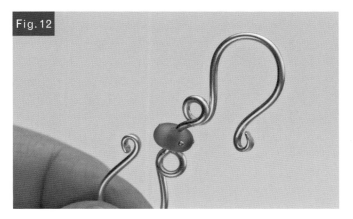

Fig. 12

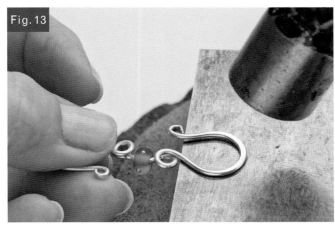

Fig. 13

7 Tumble to polish and work-harden. Note: If you are using soft stones such as pearls or turquoise, do not use the tumbler; use a polishing cloth instead.

hook clasps

Hook clasps can be utilitarian, so it was particularly fun to design some that raised the bar. Easy techniques such as coiling and hammering are a no-brainer. Using the torch and winding the wire creatively make some of these real standouts. Hook clasps are a great alternative to S-hook clasps and take only a few minutes to make.

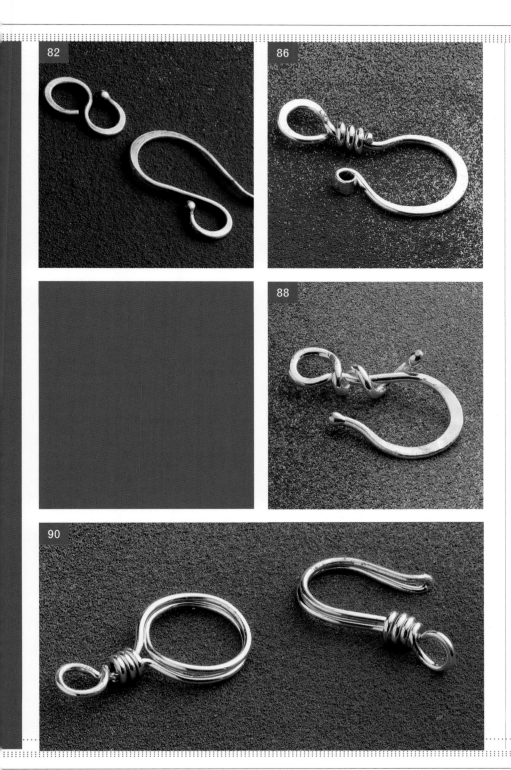

82 Ball-End Hook-and-Eye Clasp

86 Oversized Wrapped Simple Hook Clasp

88 Vine Hook Clasp

90 Double Hook-and-Eye Clasp

ball-end hook-and-eye clasp

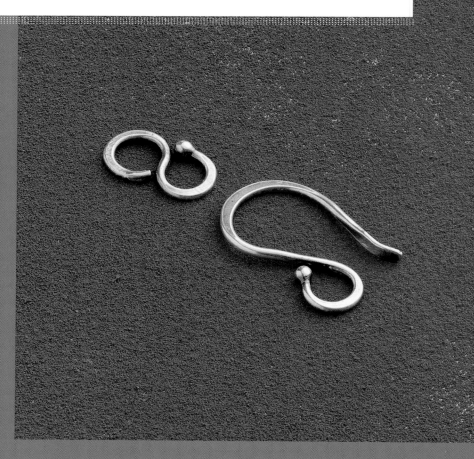

materials + tools

- 16-gauge fine silver dead-soft wire
- Fireproof work surface
- Blazer micro torch
- Fusing pliers
- Quenching bowl
- Round-nose pliers
- Flush cutters
- File or cup bur
- Ball-peen hammer
- Steel bench block
- Ruler
- Stepped (5, 7, 10 mm) forming pliers
- Rotary tumbler with mixed stainless steel shot

Finished size: ½" x ¾" (13 x 20 mm); Eye: ⁵⁄₁₆" x ½" (8 x 13 mm)

EYE

1 On a fireproof work surface, light the torch. Working off the spool, use fusing pliers to hold the end of the wire in the flame until a ball forms *(Fig. 1)*. Turn off the torch. Dip the wire in the quenching bowl to cool, then dry.

Fig. 1

2 Using the back of the round-nose pliers, grasp the wire just beneath the ball. Rotate the pliers away from you, rolling the wire completely over, forming a P-shaped loop *(Fig. 2)*. Repeat this entire step for the other half of the eye with the other end of the wire, but rolling in the opposite direction *(Fig. 3)*. Cut the wire from the spool *(Fig. 4)*. Use the file or cup bur to round the cut end of the wire. Close the loop with round-nose pliers.

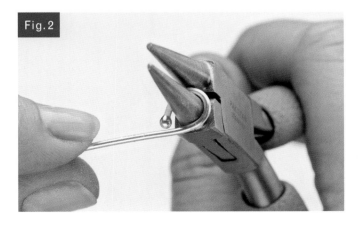

Fig. 2

Fig. 3

Fig. 4

3 Use the hammer and bench block to flatten the curve on each side of the clasp *(Fig. 5)*.

Fig. 5

HOOK

4 Repeat Step 1. Grasp the wire just below the ball with the back of the round-nose pliers and roll the pliers away from you to make a P-shaped loop *(Fig. 6)*. Measure 1½" (3.8 cm) from the loop and cut the wire from the spool *(Fig. 7)*. Round and smooth the cut end of the wire with the file or cup bur.

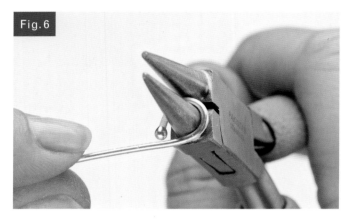
Fig. 6

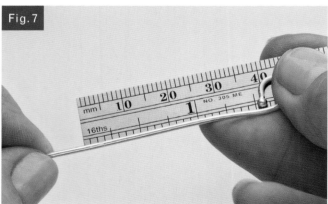
Fig. 7

5 Holding the loop perpendicular to the bench block, make a ¼" (6 mm) paddle on the cut end of the wire *(Fig. 8)*.

Fig. 8

6 Using the large (10 mm) step of the stepped pliers, grasp the wire just below the first loop and bend the wire in the opposite direction to form a hook *(Fig. 9)*. Use round-nose pliers to bend the end of the hook up slightly *(Fig. 10)*.

Fig. 9

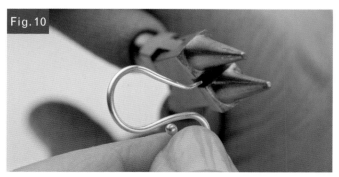
Fig. 10

7 Use the hammer and bench block to flatten the curve and loop of the clasp *(Fig. 11)*. Do not hammer the ball.

Fig. 11

If you leave a hook clasp open too wide, it will not secure your piece. Pinch it shut as much as you need in order to securely hold the jump ring you've chosen.

8 Tumble the hook-and-eye to polish and work-harden.

oversized wrapped simple hook clasp

materials + tools

- 4" (10 cm) of 16-gauge sterling silver dead-soft wire
- Flush cutters
- Chain-nose pliers
- Round-nose pliers
- Steel bench block
- Ball-peen hammer
- Ruler
- Sharpie marker
- Rotary tumbler with mixed stainless steel shot

Finished size: ⅝"x 1⅛" (1.5 x 2.8 cm)

1 Flush cut both ends of the wire. Use chain-nose pliers to make a 90° bend at the middle of the wire *(Fig. 1)*. Use the back of the round-nose pliers to make a large wrapped loop *(Fig. 2)*.

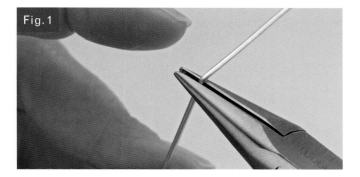

Fig. 1

Fig. 2

2 Holding the wire perpendicular to the bench block, hammer a ¼" (6 mm) paddle on the cut end of the wire *(Fig. 3)*. Use the tip of the round-nose pliers to make a small loop at the end of the paddle *(Fig. 4)*.

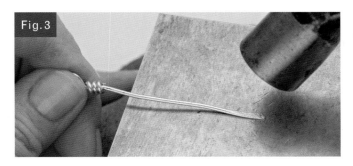

Fig. 3

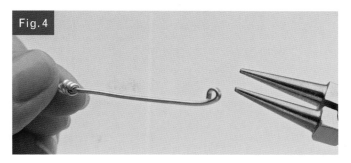

Fig. 4

3 Place the Sharpie in the middle of the length of wire and bend the wire around the marker to form a large hook *(Fig. 5)*. Use chain-nose pliers to bend the wire just above the wrap to a 45° angle *(Fig. 6)*.

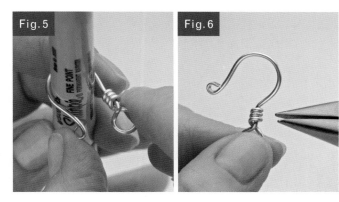

Fig. 5

Fig. 6

4 Use the hammer and bench block to flatten the top of the hook and the bottom of the loop *(Fig. 7)*.

Fig. 7

5 Tumble to polish and work-harden.

vine hook clasp

materials + tools

- 14–16-gauge fine silver dead-soft wire
- Fireproof work surface
- Blazer micro torch
- Fusing pliers
- Quenching bowl
- File
- Chain-nose pliers
- Ruler
- Round-nose pliers
- Sharpie marker
- Flush cutters
- Ball-peen hammer
- Steel bench block
- Rotary tumbler with mixed stainless steel shot

Finished size: ⅝" x 1⅛" (1.5 x 2.8 cm)

1 On a fireproof work surface, light the torch. Working from the spool, use fusing pliers to hold the end of the wire in the flame until a ball forms *(Fig. 1)*. Turn off the torch. Dip the wire in the quenching bowl to cool, then dry. File any burs if necessary.

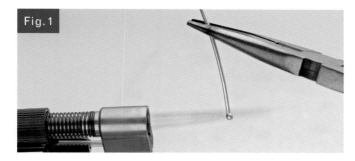
Fig. 1

2 Use chain-nose pliers to bend the wire to a 90° angle 2" (5 cm) from the ball *(Fig. 2)*. Make a loose wrapped loop using the back of the round-nose pliers *(Fig. 3)*.

Fig. 2

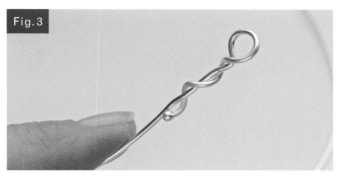
Fig. 3

3 Bend the wire around the Sharpie to form a hook *(Fig. 4)*. Cut the wire from the spool opposite the top of the loop.

Fig. 4

4 Light the torch. Open up the hook slightly and ball the end in the flame. Turn off the torch. Dip the wire in the quenching bowl to cool, then dry. File any burs if necessary. Reshape the hook with the Sharpie. Use round-nose pliers to bend the end of the hook up slightly *(Fig. 5)*.

Fig. 5

5 Flatten the curve of the hook and loop with the hammer and bench block *(Fig. 6)*.

Fig. 6

6 Tumble to polish and work-harden.

double hook-and-eye clasp

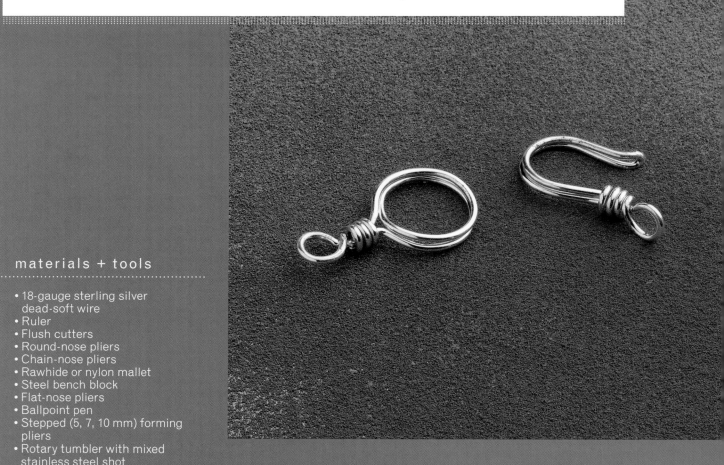

materials + tools

- 18-gauge sterling silver dead-soft wire
- Ruler
- Flush cutters
- Round-nose pliers
- Chain-nose pliers
- Rawhide or nylon mallet
- Steel bench block
- Flat-nose pliers
- Ballpoint pen
- Stepped (5, 7, 10 mm) forming pliers
- Rotary tumbler with mixed stainless steel shot

Finished size: $\frac{7}{16}$" x $\frac{7}{8}$" (11 x 22 mm); Eye: $\frac{5}{16}$" x $\frac{7}{8}$" (8 x 22 mm)

HOOK

1 Cut 5" (12.5 cm) of wire and flush cut each end. Measure 1½" (3.8 cm) from one end of the wire and create a hairpin shape with the tip of the round-nose pliers *(Fig. 1)*.

Fig. 1

2 Use chain-nose pliers to pinch the fold closed *(Fig. 2)*. If necessary, use the mallet and steel bench block to realign the wires so they are parallel to each other.

Fig. 2

3 Hold the wire so the U is at the bottom, the short wire is on the left, and the long wire is on the right *(Fig. 3)*. Use chain-nose pliers to make a 90° bend opposite the short wire *(Fig. 4)*. Use round-nose pliers to begin a wrapped loop. If necessary, trim the left core wire even with the bottom of the loop *(Fig. 5)*. Hold the core wires flat with flat-nose pliers and use chain-nose pliers to make one snug wrap. This will prevent the core wires from twisting during the wrapping. Now grasp the loop with the flat-nose pliers and continue the wrap until both

core wires are secure *(Fig. 6)*. Trim the excess wire and tuck in the tail with chain-nose pliers.

Fig. 3

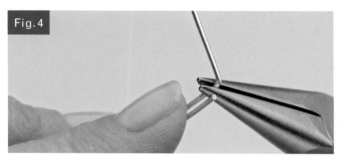

Fig. 4

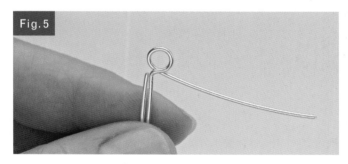

Fig. 5

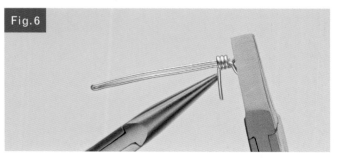

Fig. 6

4 Grasp the loop flat in the chain-nose pliers. Hold the core wires against the ballpoint pen ¼" (6 mm) from the wrap and bend the wires over the pen to form a hook *(Fig. 7)*. Use the tip of the round-nose pliers to slightly bend the end of the hook up *(Fig. 8)*. Use chain-nose pliers to bend the wires just above the wrap to a 45° angle *(Fig. 9)*.

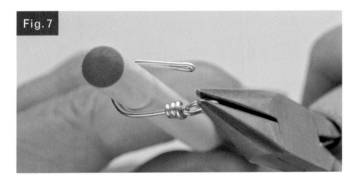

Fig. 7

Fig. 8

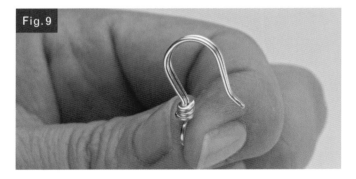

Fig. 9

EYE

5 Working from the spool, flush cut the end of the wire, then grasp the wire 3" (7.5 cm) from the end with the large (10 mm) step of the stepped pliers *(Fig. 10)*. Wrap the spool end twice around the jaw of the pliers *(Fig. 11)*. With chain-nose pliers, bend both of the straight wires to a 90° angle *(Fig. 12)*.

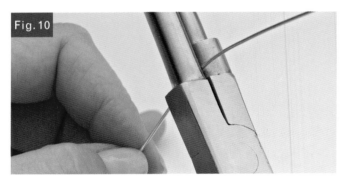

Fig. 10

Fig. 11

Fig. 12

6 Trim the spool wire to ¼" (6 mm) from the loop. Using the tip of the chain-nose pliers, grasp the long wire opposite the short wire and make a 90° bend *(Fig. 13)*. Using round-nose pliers, begin a wrapped loop with the long wire *(Fig. 14)*. Hold the loop flat in the flat-nose pliers and use chain-nose pliers to wrap the wire around both of the core wires *(Fig. 15)*. When both core wires are secure, trim the excess wire and tuck in the tail with chain-nose pliers.

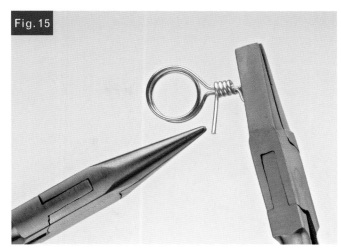

Fig. 15

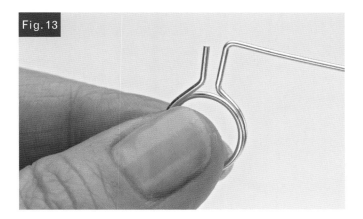

Fig. 13

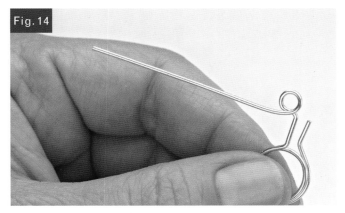

Fig. 14

7 Tumble to polish and work-harden.

toggle clasps

If you're hankering to use fire, fusing rings opens up the world of toggle clasps. (If you'd rather not use a torch, though, we've designed some that don't need flame.) All toggles consist of a ring and a bar, and attaching several links of chain to the bar makes them more flexible and easier to open and close. Toggles can be made in any size you need for your design.

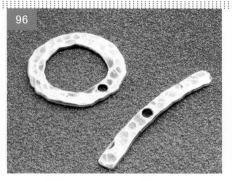

hammered toggle clasp

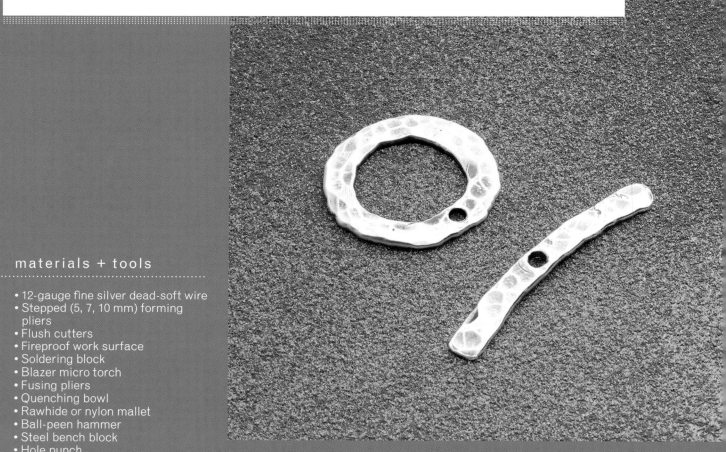

materials + tools

- 12-gauge fine silver dead-soft wire
- Stepped (5, 7, 10 mm) forming pliers
- Flush cutters
- Fireproof work surface
- Soldering block
- Blazer micro torch
- Fusing pliers
- Quenching bowl
- Rawhide or nylon mallet
- Ball-peen hammer
- Steel bench block
- Hole punch
- File
- Sharpie marker
- Liver of sulfur
- Rotary tumbler with mixed stainless steel shot

Finished size: Ring: ¾" (20 mm); Toggle: ⅛" x ⅜" (3 x 10 mm)

RING

1 Working from the spool, make a jump ring using the large (10 mm) step of the stepped pliers *(Fig. 1)*. Flush cut both ends of the wire so there is no gap when the ring is closed *(Fig. 2)*.

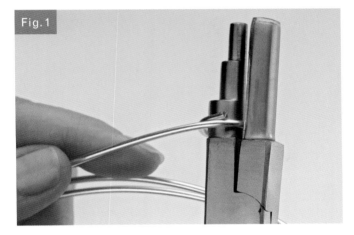
Fig. 1

Fig. 2

2 On a fireproof work surface, light the torch. Place the ring on the soldering block. Holding the torch about 1½" (3.8 cm) from the ring, rotate the flame around the ring in a circle, slowly heating the whole surface. When the ring glows, concentrate the flame on the join until it flows together *(Fig. 3)*. Turn off the torch. Use fusing pliers to dip the ring in the quenching bowl to cool, then dry.

Fig.3

3 If necessary, reshape the ring on the large step of the stepped pliers using a rawhide or nylon mallet to bring it back to round.

4 Use the ball-peen hammer and bench block to flatten the ring *(Fig. 4)*. Use the round head of the ball-peen hammer to create a dimpled effect on one side of the ring *(Fig. 5)*.

5 Punch one hole in the ring using the hole punch *(Fig. 6)*.

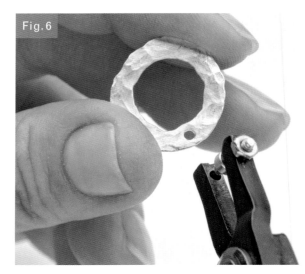

Fig. 6

Fig. 4

Fig. 5

Toggle clasps can be elegant, fun, or funky, and they're one of the easiest clasps to open and close. Finish your beautiful designs with a handcrafted clasp to truly personalize your jewelry.

Tip: When flattening wire with a hammer, work slowly and in stages. If you over-flatten the toggle bar and ring, you may end up with sharp edges. Also, never flatten overlapping wires as this weakens the wire considerably.

6 Working from the spool, measure a length of wire against the ring you just made. The wire should extend ⅛" (3 mm) beyond each side of the ring *(Fig. 7)*. Cut the wire from the spool and file the ends smooth.

Fig. 7

7 Use the ball-peen hammer and bench block to flatten the bar *(Fig. 8)*. Use the round end of the ball-peen hammer to dimple the bar *(Fig. 9)*. Mark the center of the bar with a Sharpie and punch a hole with the hole punch *(Fig. 10)*.

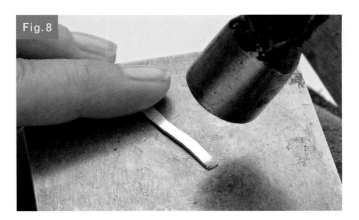

Fig. 8

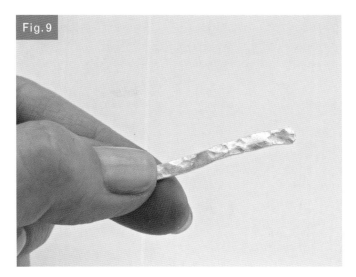

Fig. 9

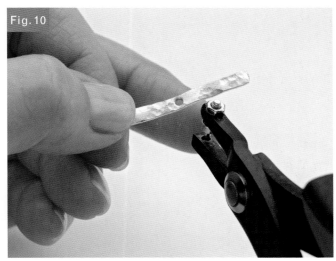

Fig. 10

8 Oxidize with liver of sulfur if desired. Tumble both pieces to polish and work-harden.

asian toggle clasp

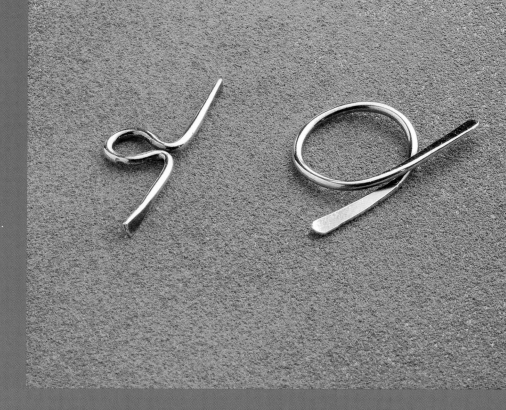

materials + tools

- 16-gauge sterling silver dead-soft wire
- Flush cutters
- Sharpie marker
- Ruler
- Ball-peen hammer
- Steel bench block
- Rawhide or nylon mallet
- File
- Round-nose pliers
- Chain-nose pliers
- Rotary tumbler with mixed stainless steel shot

Finished size: Ring: ⅝" (15 mm); Toggle: ¹⁄₁₆" x 1¹⁄₁₆" (1.5 x 27 mm)

RING

1 Working from the spool, flush cut the end of the wire. Holding the Sharpie 1½" (3.8 cm) from the cut end, cross the wires *(Fig. 1)*. Cut the wire off the spool ½" (1.3 cm) from the cross. Measure again to make sure both wires are ½" (1.3 cm) from the cross *(Fig. 2)*.

2 Gently open the ring as you would a jump ring. Use the ball-peen hammer and bench block to flatten each end of the wire into a paddle up to the cross *(Fig. 3)*. Use the rawhide or nylon mallet to reshape the ring on the Sharpie. Use the file to round the ends of the paddles *(Fig. 4)*.

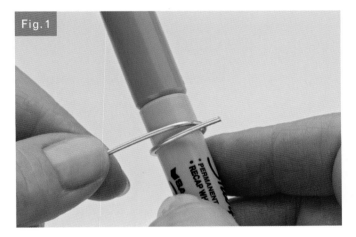

Fig. 1

Fig. 3

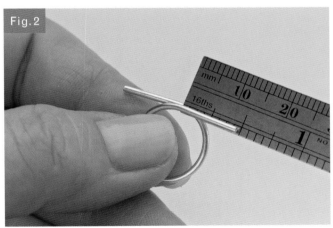

Fig. 2

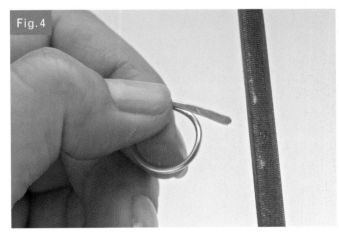

Fig. 4

TOGGLE

3 Working from the spool, flush cut the end of the wire. Wrap the wire around the middle of the round-nose pliers 1¼" (3.2 cm) from the end to make a loop *(Fig. 5)*. Measure 1" (2.5 cm) from the loop and flush cut the wire from the spool.

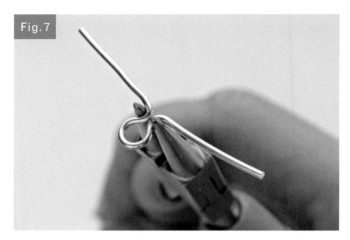

Fig. 7

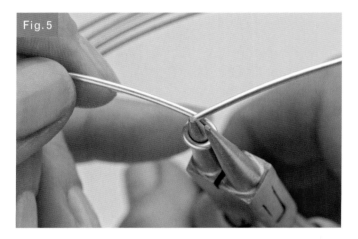

Fig. 5

4 Hold the loop with chain-nose pliers and use your fingers to bend each wire back to a 90° angle *(Fig. 6)*. Use round-nose pliers to reshape the loop if necessary, then pinch the loop to close it securely *(Fig. 7)*. Trim the ends to ½" (1.3 cm) from the bend in the loop. Use the ball-peen hammer and bench block to flatten each end into a ¼" (6 mm) paddle *(Fig. 8)*. Use the file to round the ends of the wire.

Fig. 8

5 Tumble both pieces to polish and work-harden.

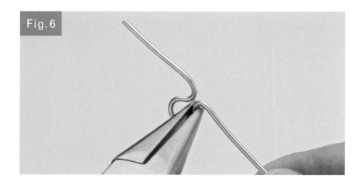

Fig. 6

Patinaed or polished? Metal looks great either way! Many of the projects in this book have been patinaed with liver of sulfur. It adds such richness and depth to the pieces, as well as being a low-maintenance addition to your designs (no tarnishing!). However, you may prefer highly polished findings. Using a rotary tumbler, stainless steel mixed-shot, warm water, and a dash of non-ultra dish soap is the easiest way to bring out the high shine in your pieces. Let the tumbler do the work! And for maintenance, use a Pro-Polish polishing pad for a quick touch-up.

When making this clasp, make sure to hammer the toggle and clasp on the right plane. The ring tips are hammered on the same plane as the ring. The toggle tips are hammered on a perpendicular plane in order for the toggle to sit properly in the ring.

twisted toggle clasp

materials + tools

- 16-gauge fine silver dead-soft wire
- 24-gauge sterling silver twisted wire
- Ruler
- Round-nose pliers
- Ring mandrel
- Flush cutters
- Fireproof work surface
- Blazer micro torch
- Soldering block
- Fusing pliers
- Quenching bowl
- Polishing cloth
- Liver of sulfur
- Rotary tumbler with mixed stainless steel shot

Finished size: Ring: ¾" (20 mm); Toggle: ¼" x 1¼" (6 x 32 mm)

RING

1 Working from the spool of 16-gauge wire, grasp 1½"
(3.8 cm) from the end with the middle of the round-nose
pliers *(Fig. 1)*. Wrap both ends of the wire around the
pliers to form a loop, ending with the wires forming a
straight line *(Fig. 2)*. Hold the loop against the size 2
mark on the ring mandrel and cross both ends over the
mandrel *(Fig. 3)*.

Fig. 3

2 Cut through both ends of the wire where they cross as if
to make a jump ring. Flush cut both ends so there is no
gap when the ring is closed *(Fig. 4)*.

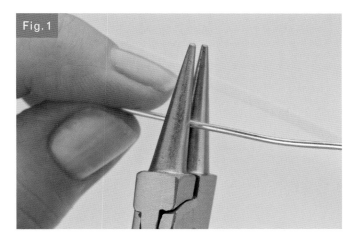

Fig. 1

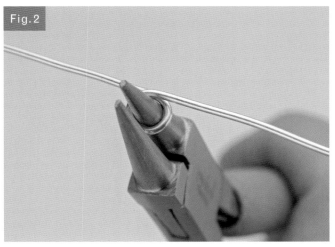

Fig. 4

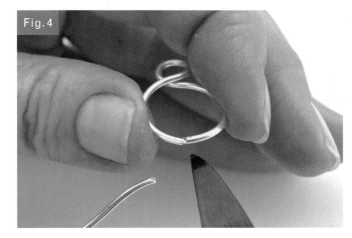

Fig. 2

3 On a fireproof work surface, light the torch. Place the ring on the soldering block. Heat the entire surface of the ring until it glows, then concentrate the flame on the join until it flows and the ends fuse together. Turn off the torch. Use fusing pliers to dip the ring in the quenching bowl to cool. Dry the ring *(Fig. 5)*. Use a file to smooth any lumps, but it doesn't have to be perfect, the ring will be covered with wire.

Fig. 5

4 Light the torch. Working from the spool of 24-gauge twisted wire, use fusing pliers to hold the end of the wire in the flame until a ball forms *(Fig. 6)*. Turn off the torch. Dip the wire in the quenching bowl, then dry. Polish the end of the wire with a polishing cloth to remove the oxidation caused by the flame *(Fig. 7)*.

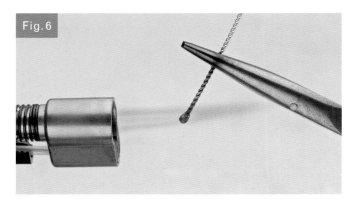

Fig. 6

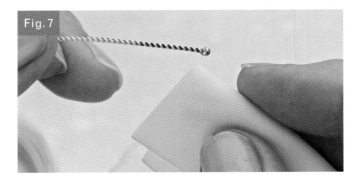

Fig. 7

5 Measure 30" (76 cm) from the ball and cut the twisted wire off the spool. With your fingers, hold the ball against the small loop and begin wrapping the wire around the large loop in neat coils *(Fig. 8)*. When you reach the end of the large loop, cut the final wrap on the inside of the ring. Use chain-nose pliers to pinch the end of the twisted wire against the loop *(Fig. 9)*.

Fig. 8

Fig. 9

6 Put the ring back on the mandrel to bring it back to round.

TOGGLE

7 Working from the spool of 16-gauge wire, grasp 1¼"
(3.2 cm) from the end with the middle of the round-nose
pliers. Wrap both ends of the wire around the pliers to
form a loop, ending with the wires forming a straight
line *(Fig. 10)*. Trim the wire to ¾" (2 cm) on each side
from the center of the loop.

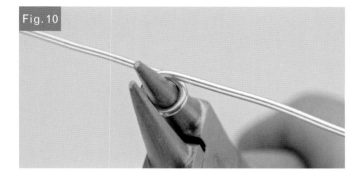

Fig. 10

8 Light the torch. Use fusing pliers to hold one end of the
toggle bar in the flame until a ball forms. Dip the wire
in the quenching bowl to cool. Repeat to create a ball
on the other end *(Fig. 11)*. Quench and dry. Ball one end
of the twisted wire left over from Step 5 (about 18" [45.5
cm]). Quench. Turn off the torch. Dry the balled end of
the twisted wire and polish with a polishing cloth to
remove the oxidation caused by the flame.

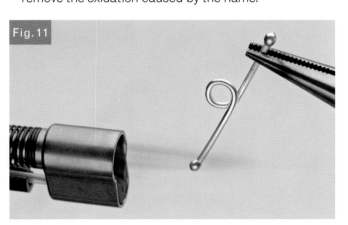

Fig. 11

9 Holding the balled end of the twisted wire next to the
loop on the bar, wrap the twisted wire around the bar
until it reaches the end *(Fig. 12)*. Trim the twisted wire
underneath the bar and pinch in the end with chain-
nose pliers *(Fig. 13)*.

Fig. 12

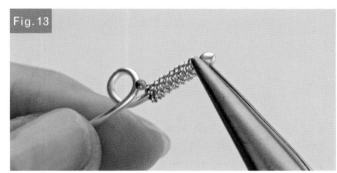

Fig. 13

10 Light the torch and ball one end of the leftover piece
of twisted wire. Quench. Turn off the torch. Dry the
wire and polish with a polishing cloth. Repeat Step 9
(Fig. 14). Oxidize with liver of sulfur, then tumble both
pieces to polish and work-harden.

Fig. 14

ball-end toggle clasp

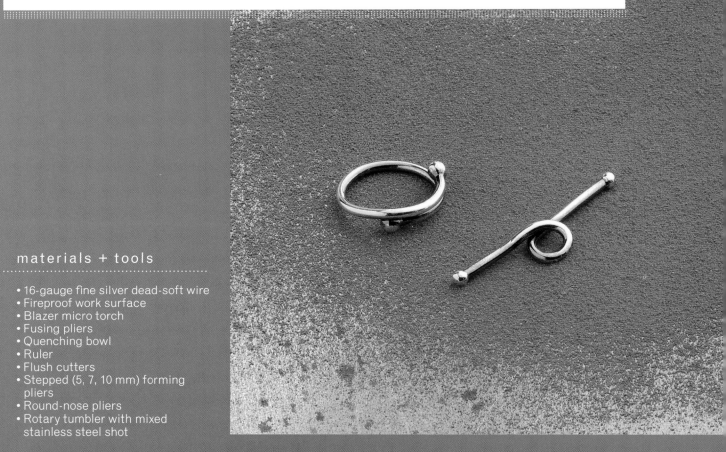

materials + tools

- 16-gauge fine silver dead-soft wire
- Fireproof work surface
- Blazer micro torch
- Fusing pliers
- Quenching bowl
- Ruler
- Flush cutters
- Stepped (5, 7, 10 mm) forming pliers
- Round-nose pliers
- Rotary tumbler with mixed stainless steel shot

Finished size: Ring: ½" (13 mm); Toggle: ¼" x 1¹⁄₁₆" (6 x 27 mm)

1 On a fireproof work surface, light the torch. Working from the spool, use the fusing pliers to hold the end of the wire in the flame until a ball forms *(Fig. 1)*. Turn off the torch. Dip the wire in the quenching bowl to cool, then dry.

Fig. 1

2 Measure 2⅜" (6 cm) from the ball and cut the wire off the spool. Light the torch. Use fusing pliers to hold the cut end of the wire in the flame until a ball forms. Quench. Turn off the torch. Dry the wire.

3 Grasp the wire right next to the ball with the large (10 mm) step of the stepped pliers and wrap the wire entirely around the jaw *(Fig. 2)*.

Fig. 2

4 Light the torch. Working from the spool, use the fusing pliers to hold the end of the wire in the flame until it forms a ball. Quench. Turn off the torch. Dry the wire.

5 Cut the wire 1¾" (4.5 cm) from the ball. Light the torch and ball the cut end of the wire *(Fig. 3)*. Quench. Turn off the torch. Dry the wire.

Fig. 3

6 Place the middle of the wire halfway down the jaws of the round-nose pliers. Wrap the wires around the jaw of the pliers in opposite directions until they form a straight bar *(Fig. 4)*.

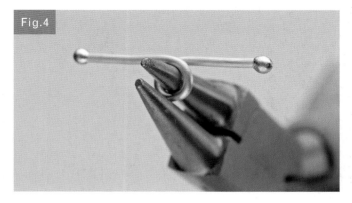

Fig. 4

7 Tumble both pieces to polish and work-harden.

lashed toggle clasp

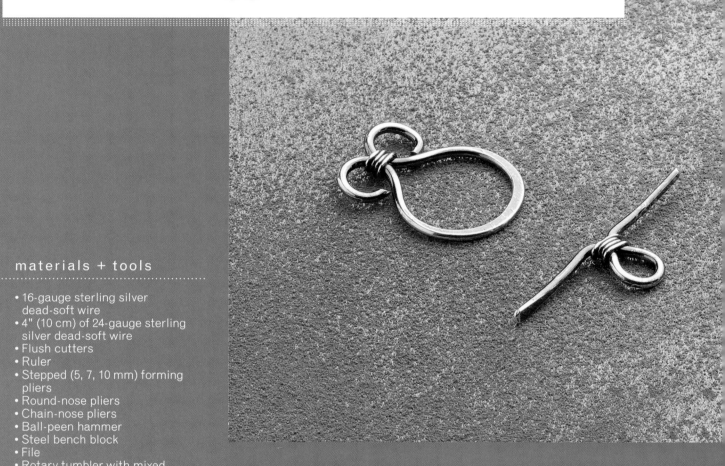

materials + tools

- 16-gauge sterling silver dead-soft wire
- 4" (10 cm) of 24-gauge sterling silver dead-soft wire
- Flush cutters
- Ruler
- Stepped (5, 7, 10 mm) forming pliers
- Round-nose pliers
- Chain-nose pliers
- Ball-peen hammer
- Steel bench block
- File
- Rotary tumbler with mixed stainless steel shot

Finished size: Toggle: 1¼" (3.2 cm); Ring: ⅝" x ⅞" (1.6 x 2.2 cm)

RING

1 Working from the spool, flush cut the end of the 16-gauge wire. Grasp the wire 1½" (3.8 cm) from the end with the large (10 mm) step of the stepped pliers *(Fig. 1)*. Bring the end of the wire around the barrel until it crosses the spool wire, forming a circle *(Fig. 2)*. Remove the wire from the pliers and trim each side to ¾" (2 cm) from where the wires cross.

Fig. 1

Fig. 2

2 Use the middle of the round-nose pliers to make a simple loop on each end of the wire, facing in opposite directions *(Fig. 3)*.

Fig. 3

3 Using your fingers, wrap 2" (5 cm) of 24-gauge wire around the neck just below the loops *(Fig. 4)*. Trim the excess wire on the back of the ring and pinch in the ends with chain-nose pliers.

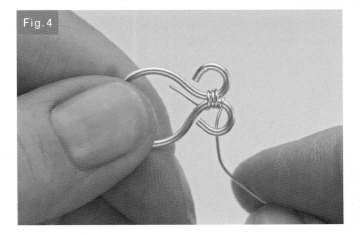

Fig. 4

4 Use the hammer and bench block to flatten the top curve of the ring *(Fig. 5)*.

Fig. 5

5 Working from the spool of 16-gauge wire, flush cut the end of the wire. Measure 1½" (3.8 cm) from the end and wrap both wires around the middle of the round-nose pliers in opposite directions to make a loop with the ends forming a straight line *(Fig. 6)*. Cut the wire off the spool 1" (2.5 cm) from the loop.

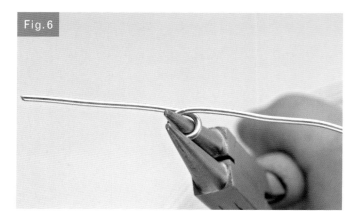

Fig. 6

6 Use chain-nose pliers to bend each wire back to a 90° angle *(Fig. 7)*. Trim the ends to ½" (1.3 cm) from the bend in the loop. Use round-nose pliers to pinch the loop and close it securely *(Fig. 8)*.

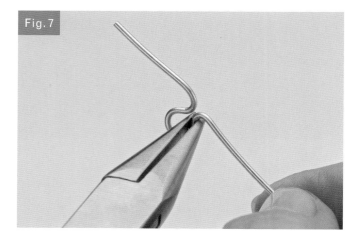

Fig. 7

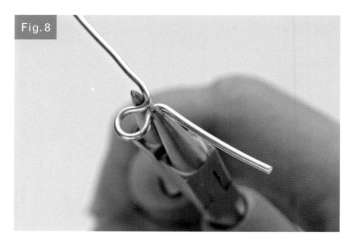

Fig. 8

7 Use the hammer and bench block to flatten the ends of the wire into a paddle *(Fig. 9)*.

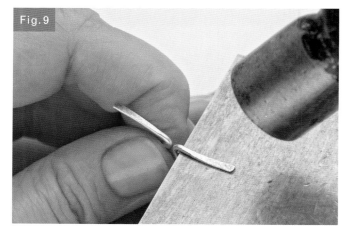

Fig. 9

8 Use the remaining 2" (5 cm) of 24-gauge wire to wrap around the neck of the loop *(Fig. 10)*. Trim the excess wire on the back of the toggle and tuck in the ends with chain-nose pliers. File the ends of the toggle to round and smooth *(Fig. 11)*.

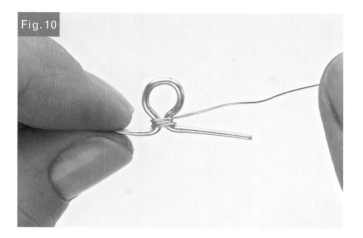
Fig. 10

Fig. 11

This clasp would look great with contrasting colored wire for the lashing. Make the piece in silver and wrap it in gold-filled wire. Or, for a more playful piece, wrap with colored craft wire. You can make an array of different clasps just by varying the type and color of wire used.

9 Tumble both pieces to polish and work-harden.

decorative balls toggle clasp

materials + tools

- 12-gauge fine silver dead-soft wire
- 18-gauge fine silver wire
- 14-gauge fine silver dead-soft wire
- Ring mandrel
- Flush cutters
- File
- Fireproof work surface
- Blazer micro torch
- Soldering block
- Fusing pliers
- Quenching bowl
- Ball-peen hammer
- Steel bench block
- Rawhide or nylon mallet
- Toothpick
- Honey or flux
- Tweezers
- Liver of sulfur
- Rotary tumbler with mixed stainless steel shot

Finished size: Ring: ⅞" (21.5 mm);
Toggle: ⅛" x 1⅓" (3 x 35 mm)

RING

1 Working from the spool of 12-gauge wire, wrap the wire around the size 6 mark on the ring mandrel to make a jump ring *(Fig. 1)*. Flush cut and file the ends of the wire so they meet with no gap.

Fig. 3

Fig. 1

2 Place the ring on the soldering block and light the torch. Holding the torch about 1½" (3.8 cm) from the ring, rotate the flame around the ring in a circle, slowly heating the whole surface. When the ring glows, concentrate the flame on the join until it flows together *(Fig. 2)*. Turn off the torch. Use fusing pliers to dip the ring in the quenching bowl to cool, then dry.

Fig. 4

3 If necessary, reshape the ring on the mandrel using a rawhide or nylon mallet *(Fig. 3)*.

4 Use the ball-peen hammer and bench block to hammer the ring flat *(Fig. 4)*. Set aside.

Fig. 2

BALLS

5 Cut the 18-gauge wire into five ⅜" (1 cm) snippets. Spread out the pieces on the soldering block *(Fig. 5)*. Light the torch and heat the pieces until each forms a ball *(Fig. 6)*. Turn off the torch. Use the fusing pliers to dip each ball in the quenching bowl to cool, then dry.

Fig. 8

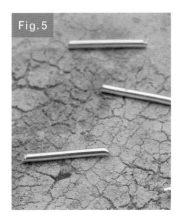
Fig. 5

Fig. 6

Fig. 9

Fig. 7

6 Place the ring from Step 4 on the soldering block. Use the toothpick to place 3 drops of honey or flux on the flattened ring where you would like the balls to be attached *(Fig. 7)*. Use tweezers to place the balls on the honey or flux *(Fig. 8)*.

7 Light the torch. Starting with a medium flame and the torch about 4" (10 cm) from the ring, rotate the flame around the ring to gently heat the entire surface. If a ball falls off the ring, replace it and begin again. When the flux or honey stops bubbling, move the torch closer to the ring and rotate it around the ring until both the ring and the balls glow. Keep the torch moving until the ring and balls fuse together *(Fig. 9)*. *Be careful not to hold the flame too close to the balls or they will completely melt into the ring.* Turn off the torch. Use fusing pliers to dip the ring in the quenching bowl to cool, then dry. File any burs if necessary.

8 Working from the spool of 14-gauge wire, flush cut the end, then grasp the wire 1" (2.5 cm) from the end with the tip of the round-nose pliers. Wrap both sides of the wire around the jaw, crossing them until they form a straight bar *(Fig. 10)*. Cut the wire off the spool, leaving ⅝" (1.5 cm) from the loop. Trim the other side of the bar to the same length.

9 Use the hammer and bench block to flatten each end of the toggle into a paddle *(Fig. 11)*. Use the file to round each end.

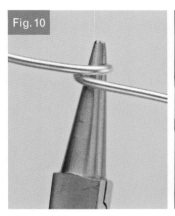
Fig. 10

Fig. 11

10 Use fusing pliers to dig a trough in the soldering block to hold the loop of the toggle bar flat on the block. Using a toothpick, place a tiny drop of honey or flux near the end of one paddle where you want to attach a ball *(Fig. 12)*. Use tweezers to place the ball on the drop of honey. Light the torch. Starting with the torch about 4" (10 cm) from the toggle, gently heat the ball end of the toggle. When the flux or honey stops bubbling, move the torch closer to the toggle and move it back and forth until both the paddle and the ball glow. Keep the torch moving until the paddle and ball fuse together *(Fig. 13)*.

Be careful not to hold the flame too close to the ball or it will completely melt into the toggle. Use fusing pliers to dip the bar in the quenching bowl to cool. Repeat this entire step for the other end of the bar. Dry the bar.

11 File any burs if necessary. Oxidize if desired. Tumble both pieces to polish and work-harden.

Fig. 12

Fig. 13

extras

We couldn't resist sharing these last two projects with you. Wire elements can be unexpected—a real eye-catcher. Use these as a jumping-off point and experiment with your own wire designs.

120 Ribbon Bail

122 Knot Spacer

ribbon bail

materials + tools

- 5" (12.5 cm) of 16-gauge fine silver dead-soft wire
- Ball-peen hammer
- Steel bench block
- Small round needle file
- Round-nose pliers
- Liver of sulfur
- Rotary tumbler with mixed stainless steel shot

Finished size: Varies

1 Use the hammer and bench block to flatten the wire *(Fig. 1)*. File the ends smooth.

Fig. 1

2 Leaving a 1" (2.5 cm) tail, use your fingers to wrap the long end twice around the needle file *(Fig. 2)*. Bring the wire down the front of the file ½" (1.3 cm) and up the back of the file, forming a V shape *(Fig. 3)*. Continue to wrap twice around the file and leave the tail hanging down *(Fig. 4)*. Remove the bail from the file.

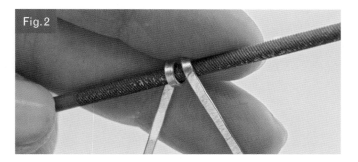
Fig. 2

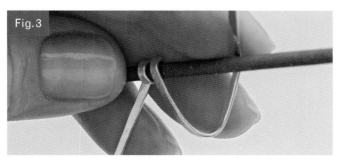
Fig. 3

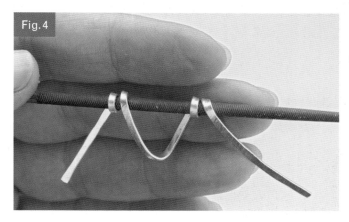
Fig. 4

3 Using the tip of the round-nose pliers, coil the ends slightly as you would a ribbon *(Fig. 5)*.

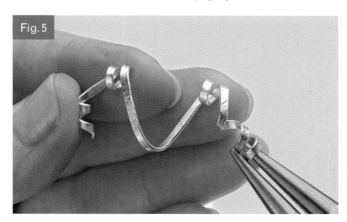
Fig. 5

4 Oxidize with liver of sulfur if desired, then tumble to polish and work-harden.

knot spacer

materials + tools

- 18-gauge sterling silver dead-soft wire or copper wire
- Flush cutters
- Stepped (5, 7, 10 mm) forming pliers
- File
- Chain-nose pliers
- Liver of sulfur
- Rotary tumbler with mixed stainless steel shot

Finished size: Varies

1 Working off the spool, flush cut the end of the wire. Grasp the tip of the wire with the second (7 mm) step of the stepped pliers. Rotate the pliers, keeping each subsequent wrap toward the back of the pliers *(Fig. 1)*. Make a coil 4 wraps long. Flush cut the wire directly across from the other end of the wire *(Fig. 2)*. File both ends. Repeat this entire step for a second coil.

Fig. 1

Fig. 2

2 With chain-nose pliers, gently open one coil enough to thread it onto the other coil *(Fig. 3)*. Continue threading the coil until it sits fully inside the other *(Fig. 4)*.

Fig. 3

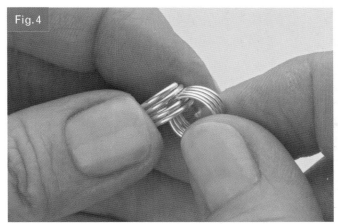

Fig. 4

3 Oxidize with liver of sulfur if desired, then tumble to polish and work-harden.

gallery

S-Clasp with Bead

Twisted Toggle Clasp

Ribbon Bail

Figure-Eight Link, Decorative Fused Ring,
Twisted Link with Bead

Tumbleweed French Ear Wires

Textured Corkscrew Link, Knot Spacer

resources

Rio Grande

riogrande.com

Round wire, mixed stainless steel shot, torch, and tools

Thunderbird Supply

thunderbirdsupply.com

Twisted wire

Harbor Freight Tools

harborfreight.com

Rotary tumbler and tools

Metalliferous

metalliferous.com

Wire and tools

Beaducation

beaducation.com

Tools and stamps

index

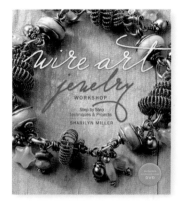